The Honour and Grandeur

REGALIA, GOLD AND SILVER
AT THE MANSION HOUSE

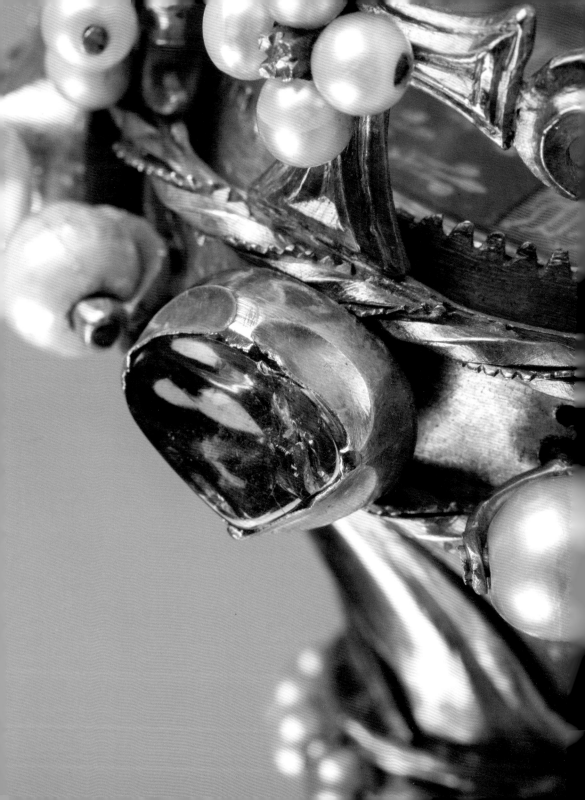

The Honour and Grandeur

REGALIA, GOLD AND SILVER
AT THE MANSION HOUSE

Michael Hall and Ralph Holt

with an introduction
by Clare Gifford

CITY
OF
LONDON

Paul Holberton publishing

ISBN 978 1 907372 89 6

British Library Cataloguing in Publication Data
A catalogue record for this book is available from the British Library

Produced by Paul Holberton publishing,
89 Borough High Street, London SE1 1NL
www.paul-holberton.net

Designed by Laura Parker

Origination and printing by E-graphic, Verona, Italy

FRONT COVER *The Crystal Sceptre, c. 1380 and c. 1420* (no. 1), detail
BACK COVER *The Brass Crosby Cup and Cover, 1772–73* (no. 18), detail
FRONTISPIECE *The Crystal Sceptre, c. 1380 and c. 1420* (no. 1), detail

CONTENTS

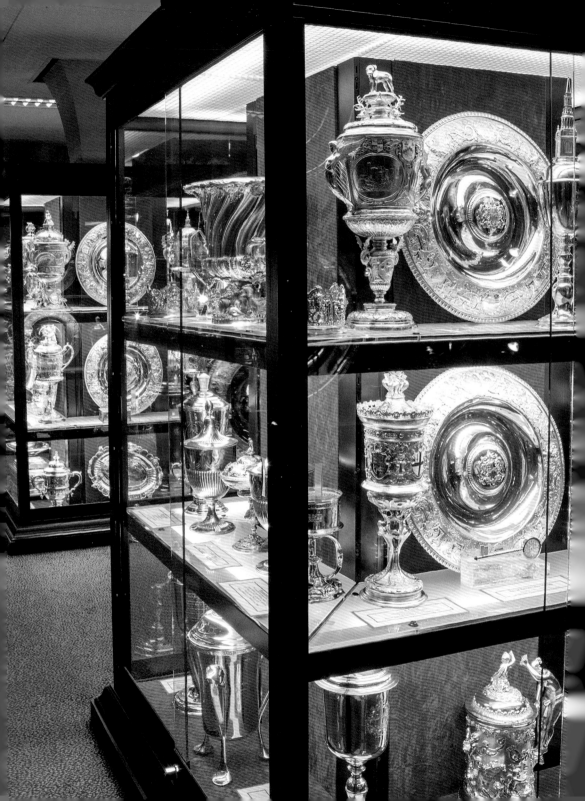

Foreword

IT IS A GREAT PLEASURE to introduce this book on the Mayoral regalia and gold and silver collection, completing the triptych of books cataloguing the treasures of the Mansion House.

The Mansion House plate collection tells a fascinating tale of Lord Mayors and their times over several centuries, the earliest item dating from *c.* 1420, and the most recent being contemporary pieces from the twenty-first century. Many of these eclectic and sometimes eccentric items are part of the day-to-day ceremonial or domestic life of each Lord Mayor and Lady Mayoress, yet this is the first time they have been photographed and their stories told for a wider audience.

Research for this book by its authors Michael Hall and Ralph Holt revealed that the Crystal Sceptre was a gift from King Henry V to the City of London following the victory at Agincourt, a battle which had been largely funded by the City. Symbolic of the City's relationship with the monarchy, this Sceptre has played a role in the solemn swearing in of each Lord Mayor at the Silent Ceremony for nearly 600 years, and is carried by the Lord Mayor at coronations.

The publication of this book is timed to accompany the first ever public exhibition of the Crystal Sceptre, which takes place on the occasion of the 600-year anniversary of the Battle of Agincourt.

I and my wife Clare, who has been behind the creation of the book and exhibition, hope that you will enjoy learning more about this incredible collection of gold and silver and how it represents this great City.

SIR ROGER GIFFORD
Lord Mayor 2012–13

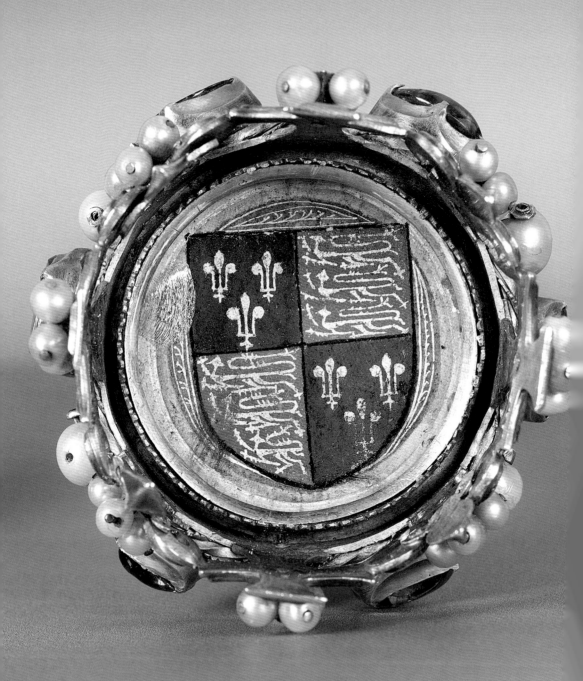

Introduction: The Crystal Sceptre

MICHAEL HALL

THE GREATEST TREASURE of the City of London has been, until now, the least known. The Crystal Sceptre (no. 1), rarely seen and never photographed before, is here presented with as much as is known of its history, its materials and their origins and its first recorded outing, to the coronation of Catherine of Valois, the wife of King Henry V, in 1421 at Westminster Abbey. For nearly 600 years the City has guarded its great jewel at the Guildhall, through the destructive Commonwealth, when symbols of royalty and the crown jewels themselves were broken up and sold, and through the two destructions of the Guildhall itself – at the Great Fire of 1666 and again in the Blitz of December 1940. Though not undamaged by time and use, the Sceptre has remained relatively unscathed. It lost the central facetted boss of crystal in the early nineteenth century, with a replacement being made of glass; the crown has been clumsily repaired and the gold of the head of the shaft shows signs of splitting; but for a fifteenth-century object such events are expected. There may well also have been enamel rosettes behind the larger pearls of the crown, now lost. The very fact it is still here, in the successor hands of those to whom it was presented, is a miracle, as no other gold and jewelled object from this period – and several have survived – have remained with their heritors.

Within the circle of the crown are set the royal arms of England, first used by Henry V from 1406 when the numbers of fleurs-de-lis were reduced to three. The artist was an Englishman, identifiable from his distinctive method of painting the heraldic lions as having also worked for the King's brother, Humphrey, Duke of Gloucester, and who probably had his scriptorium by St Paul's Cathedral. This allows us to assume that though several of the elements, like the crown and the carved rock crystals, were probably made in France, the Sceptre itself was put together in England. The crown, almost certainly made in Paris, is so small as to be useless as a human ornament, and most likely came from a votive statue of the Virgin, while the crystals are also probably of Parisian workmanship as well. How and when these elements arrived in London is unknown, but there are certainly several significant moments between Henry V's accession in 1406 and 1421 when they may have done so. King Sigismund of Bohemia, King of Rome and eventually Holy Roman Emperor, visited England for several months in 1416, coming through Paris on his travels. William, Count of Hainault,

The arms of Henry V from the head of the Crystal Sceptre, gouache on vellum, c. 1420

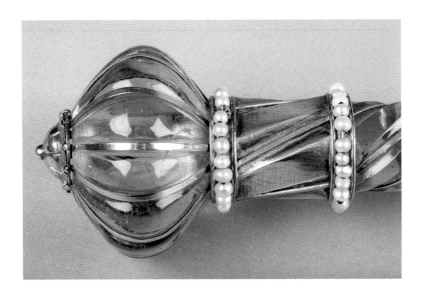

brother-in-law of the Duke of Burgundy, came in the same year, events that would
have involved lavish gift-giving and receiving. Henry V had also spent a great deal
of time in France, pursuing his claim to that throne and, though Catherine of Valois
was married without a dowry of any significance, the King would have had access
to many similar treasures whilst abroad. However, it is the links between a Lord
Mayor of London and the Archbishop of Canterbury that might account for the
joining of these various elements – the brothers Henry Chichele, Archbishop from
1414 until his death in 1443 and Robert Chichele, Lord Mayor in 1411-12 and again
in 1422-23. Archbishop Chichele owned a silver-gilt and rock-crystal salt of probably
Burgundian origin and a pair of magnificent spirally fluted Parisian flagons in
silver-gilt, elements that have echoes in the Sceptre and are now preserved in
Oxford.

The Sceptre is the only English treasure of its kind to survive in this country,
though there are several similar and related objects in treasuries and museums across
Europe. The Reliquary of the Crown of Thorns in the Waddesdon Bequest at the
British Museum, made in the 1390s for the Duke of Burgundy, only came to England
in the late nineteenth century, while a French crown made in Paris for the wife of
Richard II in the 1370s and altered in London in 1406 is now in Munich. But these are
deeply rare survivors and well known. Their ranks, along with similar works like the
Golden Horse of Allotting and the Reliquary of the True Cross at Esztergom, are now
joined by the Crystal Sceptre. The English, French and Burgundian royal inventories
of the period give graphic details of similar objects, all now sadly lost.

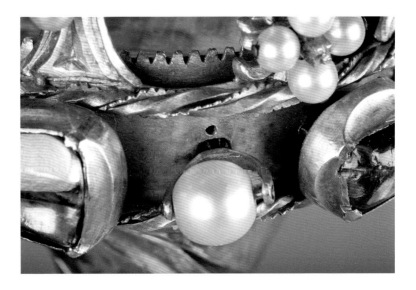

A sapphire, pearl and spinel from the crown of the Sceptre

Until now the silver-gilt Hedon Mace was believed to be the earliest surviving civic ornament in Britain. An iron weapon - a real mace - was sheathed in silver and a flared head surmounted by a crown in a plain version of the Sceptre. Hedon, by Hull in Yorkshire, received a new charter from Henry V in 1415 and as the mace bears the King's cypher it was believed to be contemporary with the grant. However, in the months after the coronation of Queen Catherine the newly-weds made a progress to the north, arriving in York by April 1423. From there the King made a pilgrimage to the shrines of St John of Bridlington and St John of Beverley. St John of Bridlington was one of the three saints the King invoked in his will before the Battle of Agincourt. The 25 October was not only the feast of St Crispin but also the feast of the Translation of St John of Beverley. Henry V, travelling from Beverley to meet the Queen in Lincoln, may well have crossed the Humber from Hedon in mid April 1423, an ideal opportunity to present the town with their mace.

Henry V, though famous as a soldier and statesman, also brought a new form of Englishness to the fore, the use of the vernacular language into government and literature. Letters to and from the Corporation of the City of London to the King and his replies were now written in English. After August 1417 Henry's signet letters, often in his own hand and previously all written in French, were now exclusively in English. In 1422 the Brewers' Company decided to record their proceedings in English, the first City livery company to do so, and soon others followed suit. The effect of the King's use of his native language had far-reaching effects on English language and literature.

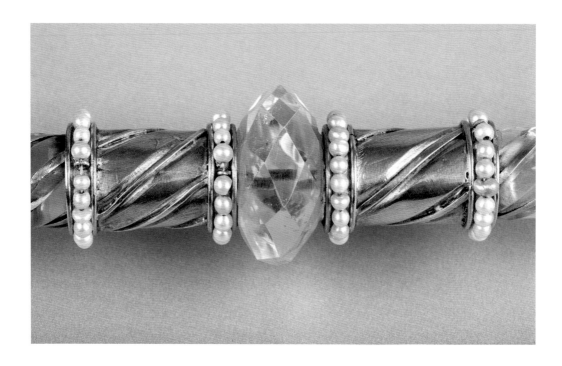

The nineteenth-century glass replacement from the centre of the Sceptre

The King restored the currency as well at a time when specie was in short supply and having a deleterious effect on the economy. Though the City raised much needed finance for the French wars against the security of the King's treasure - Richard Whittington and Robert Chichele being amongst the greatest lenders - the King took direct action to improve the flow of coinage. He re-opened the ancient Roman tin and silver mines at Combe Martin on the north Devon coast and much of the surviving Henrician coinage is made from Devonshire silver. The Mansion House plate collection has a curious reminder of this source of silver, as the Elizabethan entrepreneur Sir Bevis Bulmer again mined at Combe Martin and presented the City with a Devonshire silver bowl in 1594 (see no. 13). Remade several times, the three tankards that resulted are of the same high silver content as Henry V's coinage.

More than a hundred years were to pass before the City received their second greatest surviving treasure, the Chain of Esses (no. 2), made in the reign of another Henry. As each Lord Mayor comes into office he signs an indenture to acknowledge the receipt of the City plate, a custom that still exists. From these early indentures we can see that though there was no permanent home for the Mayoralty there was some silver provided for the office. Constant wear and tear led to constant remaking and some of the silver now at Mansion House, besides the Bulmer bowl, can trace its origins to late medieval pieces (see no. 11). However, bar the Fire Cup (no. 9), a rare survivor, it was only after a permanent home was provided for the Lord Mayor, his regalia and plate, that the collection began to be formed and kept.

Mansion House was built on the site of Stocks Market between 1739 and 1752. Until the later date Lord Mayors had been seated and entertained from the livery halls of their companies, or at their own houses. If silver were given to or offered by a Lord Mayor it would have been passed to those livery companies or kept for his personal use. Hence it is to the treasuries of the livery companies that we need to look for early masterpieces of English silver relating to the City. The dreadful Sir Thomas Bludworth, Lord Mayor during the Great Fire, disappeared for the first two days of the disaster, time spent saving his own effects and probably the City treasure from his mansion by St Paul's. Only from the mid-eighteenth century could Mansion House begin to build up a collection of plate for entertaining and ceremonial use.

Though it is only possible here to present a fraction of the collection, the choice has been dictated by both the quality of the pieces and the light they cast on the part silver plays in the life of the Lord Mayor. While Lord Mayor Perry offered State dinners to ten or at the most twenty officers and Aldermen in 1739, by the time the Egyptian Hall at Mansion House was in use several hundred guests could be seated. On State occasions not only would plate be borrowed from the livery companies or hired from silversmiths, but decorations for the tables would have been largely ephemeral – marzipan and sugar sculptures in particular. The commissioning of the vast set of plates and serving dishes from Paul de Lamerie (no. 14) marks the start of the acquisition of silver suitable for the greatest city in the land.

The plate collection at Mansion House reflects both the styles of the period, the most fashionable and impressive, but also the changing uses to which silver is put, from the practical to the need to awe and impress, to commemorate great events and sooth fragile egos. Nevertheless it is all, as the inscription of the Irish Cup (no. 16) reminds us, intended for ... *the honour and grandeur of this City.*

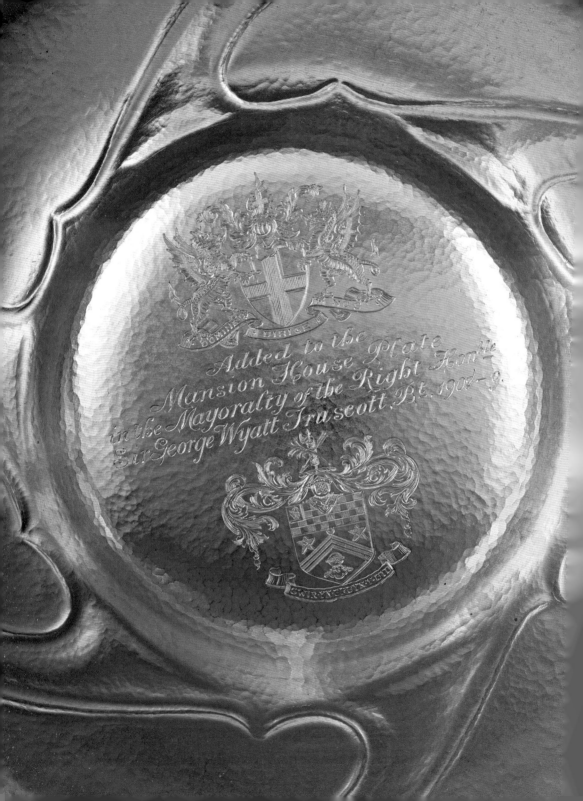

Added to the
Mansion House Plate
in the Mayoralty of the Right Hon.ble
Sir George Wyatt Truscott, Bt. 190?-9.

DOMINE DIRIGE NOS

The Regalia and Plate in Use

CLARE GIFFORD

THE MAIN WORK OF THE LORD MAYOR OF LONDON is as the principal ambassador for the City as a global financial centre, with one third of the year spent abroad 'selling' the City of London. The Lord Mayor and some of his regalia, however, are perhaps more familiar to the public through the ceremonial occasions that take place within the 'Square Mile'. The golden carriage used in the Lord Mayor's Show to travel to the Royal Courts of Justice, the ermine-trimmed gown worn on State occasions, the black and gold gown, the fabulous Chain of Esses (no. 2) and the exquisite badge of office (no. 3) can be seen regularly in newspaper and magazine coverage of major pubic occasions or official City banquets.

Ceremonial occasions within the City, such as services in St Paul's Cathedral, civic or livery events, require the Lord Mayor to be preceded by the City Sword and Mace (nos. 5 and 7), carried by the Swordbearer and the Mace Bearer. They are then mounted on the wall above the Lord Mayor's chair at banquets in the Mansion House and Guildhall, and on a table in front of the Lord Mayor when in St Paul's Cathedral.

For State occasions when Her Majesty the Queen attends, the Lord Mayor carries the Pearl Sword (no. 4) and walks ahead of the Queen whilst she is in the City. Most recently the Pearl Sword has been carried at the service to mark the end of combat in Afghanistan, the Order of the British Empire service, the Queen's Diamond Jubilee, and the service to mark the end of service operations in Iraq.

Very occasionally, only for a State funeral, a Lord Mayor may be required to escort the monarch, bearing the Mourning Sword (fig. 6). This was most recently carried at the funeral of Baroness Thatcher in May 2013, and prior to that at Sir Winston Churchill's funeral in January 1965 and Lord Nelson's funeral in January 1806.

To be integral to these historic and ceremonial events taking place in the modern City of London is a huge privilege, and one which no Lord Mayor could ever forget. But another remarkable aspect of spending a year in the voluntary civic office of Lord Mayor (and Lady Mayoress) of London is to have the extraordinary experience of living in Mansion House. This is a Georgian town palace of great opulence, exquisitely decorated and elegantly furnished with bespoke Sheraton furniture and the stately gilded Nile Suite of chairs and sofas made in 1803 to commemorate Nelson's sea victories. The house was endowed in 1987 with the Harold Samuel collection of eighty-

*Detail of the rosewater dish
(no. 56), presented by Sir George
Truscott, Bt (LM 1908–09)*

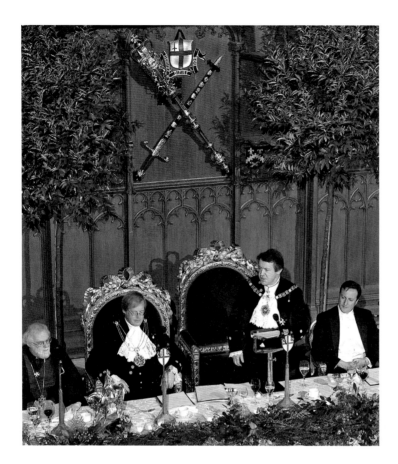

four Dutch and Flemish seventeenth-century paintings by the masters of the era,
which remain as spellbinding after living with them for a year as they are when first
encountered. Then there are the larger-than-life-sized marble statues of great classical
and literary figures in the golden niches of the Egyptian Hall, commissioned by the
City of London after the Great Exhibition in 1851 from the finest sculptors of the day.

The sense of grandeur in the Mansion House is further enhanced by the sumptuous
and historic gold and silver plate used for banquets and dining. It is remarkable to eat
and drink amongst branched candelabra, ornate cups and goblets, and the sometimes
eccentric silver-gilt gifts from visiting dignitaries to past Lord Mayors. However, it
is the very fact that these wonderful objects are in everyday use that allows them to
permeate and colour the experience of being part of the Mansion House household for
a year.

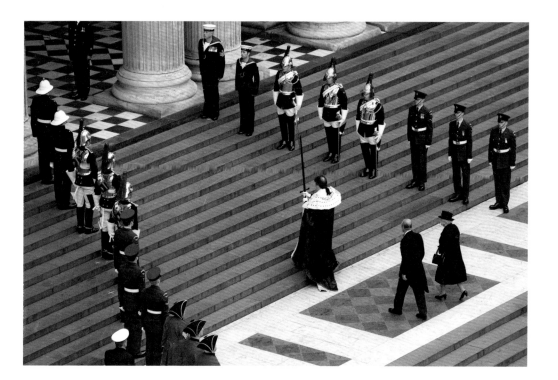

At first the items all seem part of a whole – 'the Mansion House plate collection' – and no one item is memorable as the overall effect is so overwhelming. But dining in this fairy-tale setting night after night for a year allows time to get to know some of the stories behind the items – the reasons behind the gifts given, something about the designer or maker, or the intention behind the design itself. After many evenings spent looking at the intricate designs and inscriptions, the quirks and eccentricities, the details and aesthetics of some of the pieces begin to have an effect.

Some have a special resonance with the involvements of current Lord Mayors, such as the Treloar Cup (no. 54), a beautiful gold cup presented to past Lord Mayor Treloar. He founded the Treloar Trust, which supports a school and college for severely disabled children of which every Lord Mayor is a trustee. It is a moving highlight among the Lord Mayor's civic duties to visit the school and see the support it gives the young people in its care. The Epping Forest Testimonial (no. 35), with its twisting branches, leaves and stags, commemorates the Epping Forest Act, whereby the City of London took over the Forest – and is an elegant reminder that the management of some of London's most important open spaces remains part of what the City offers the wider community in London.

The Lord Mayor Roger Gifford bearing the Mourning Sword, leading Her Majesty the Queen and the Duke of Edinburgh into St Paul's Cathedral for the funeral service of Baroness Thatcher, May 2013

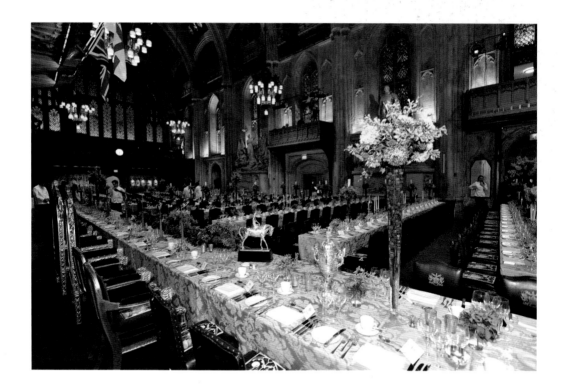

The details on some of the cups are incredible – the coiled snakes on the lids of Sir John Eamer's sauce tureens (no. 26), the Welsh harp handles of the Castle Baynard Cup (no. 43), and of course the recurring theme of City dragons, with particularly fine examples in the handles of the Oliver Cup (no. 19). There are some wonderful human figures to be found, for instance the beautiful mother-and-child relief on the Studd Cup (no. 28), the limbless men with crutches on the Cripplegate Cup (no. 37), and the little bootmakers seated at the foot of the splendid Cordwainer Cup (no. 39).

During the course of the year, favourites among these objects emerge, and it is fun to anticipate what might have been placed on the top table for the evening. Particularly fine are two pieces by Latino Movio, whose foliage and insects on the rosewater dish (no. 56) and Johnston Cup (no. 50) are so accurate and naturalistic that it is almost impossible to imagine how these were hammered into the silver by hand.

Many civic and livery dinners include the drinking of a 'loving cup' after dinner, when the toastmaster will shout from behind the Lord Mayor's chair or that of the Master of the livery company: "The Lord Mayor (or the Master) drinks to you in a loving cup and bids you all a hearty welcome!" This is an ancient ceremony arising to ensure that drinkers are protected from treachery – unlike King Edward, who

The Guildhall laid for a Banquet with the Mansion House plate collection on the tables

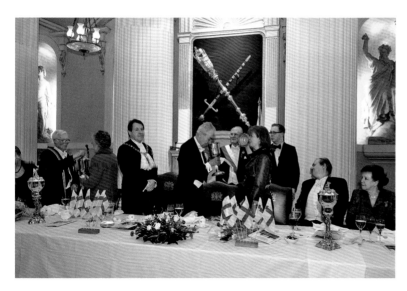

The sharing of a loving cup
in the Mansion House at the
dinner for the Order of St George

was assassinated at Corfe Castle in 978, allegedly while drinking. A silver or silver-gilt cup and cover is used, filled with spiced wine, immemorially termed 'sack'. The cups are passed round the tables and each person, after he or she has drunk, applies the napkin to the lip of the cup before passing it to their neighbour. While the drinker is occupied, a neighbour on one side stands holding the cover of the cup in the right or 'dagger' hand and the neighbour on the other side remains standing to protect the drinker.

The context of the gifts given and received seems more relevant as the year progresses. Visiting Heads of State and ministers will often present the Lord Mayor with a suitable memento – such as the model of the Al Masmak Fort given by King Abdullah of Saudi Arabia (no. 82) – whilst the Lord Mayor of London presents a large silver presentation casket with two dragons. When travelling abroad the Lord Mayor gives a smaller, single silver dragon. It is interesting to imagine the collections of gold and silver gifts collected over the decades in equivalent residences around the world. Since the Lord Mayor visits some of the same key countries with interests in the City of London each year, perhaps the presidents and ministers find themselves custodians of serried ranks of silver dragons.

The objects range from the most familiar and most frequently displayed, such as the gilt model of the Great Harry (no. 62) and the equestrian model of Princess Elizabeth (no. 73) to intriguing items which are rarely seen, such as the beautifully mounted piece of the Atlantic Cable, the laying of which was commemorated in 1866 with a grand dinner.

Some items are seen in other contexts, such as the Temple Bar inkstand (no. 57), which resides in the Lord Mayor's private office, the Venetian Parlour, and the Crystal Palace inkstand (no. 61), which officiates at the Silent Ceremony in Guildhall each November.

The Crystal Sceptre

Most spectacular of all the wonderful pieces in this book is the Crystal Sceptre (no. 1), a priceless and ancient gold and jewelled mace which is used in the Silent Ceremony as the new Lord Mayor is sworn in, to represent authority and allegiance to the Crown.

The Sceptre is also carried by the Lord Mayor of London at coronations, so it last left the Guildhall on 2 June 1953, in the safe custody of Sir Rupert de la Bère, for the coronation of Queen Elizabeth II. It has never been closely studied or photographed before, nor has it been made available for the public to view. The most recent description, accompanied by an engraving, was in 1895.

The mace is a stunningly beautiful and ancient jewel – and it is in extraordinarily good condition, having been kept as a 'working' part of the Lord Mayoral regalia for nearly 600 years. This is the first time that its fascinating history has been traced. Though the date of its acquisition by the City of London is not known or recorded for certain, it can be safely assumed to have been acquired between 1419 and 1421. In 1419 Lord Mayor Richard Whittington's *Liber Albus*, the 'White Book' of the City of London, recorded the ceremony held at the Guildhall by which the mayoralty passed from holder to holder, the precursor of the Silent Ceremony. In this description the Crystal Sceptre does not appear. However, in 1421 a mace is carried by the Lord Mayor at the coronation of Catherine of Valois, daughter of Charles VI of France and wife of Henry V. Married in France in the previous year to cement the peace of the Treaty of Troyes after the Battle of Agincourt, Catherine was crowned Queen Consort at Westminster Abbey on 23 February 1421.

Henry V knew from his father's reign that successful war needed proper funding, and he worked hard to increase income to the Exchequer in the lead-up to Agincourt. He had good relations with Parliament and was able to increase taxation, though he was unable to call on the banking families of Italy as they had been ruined by

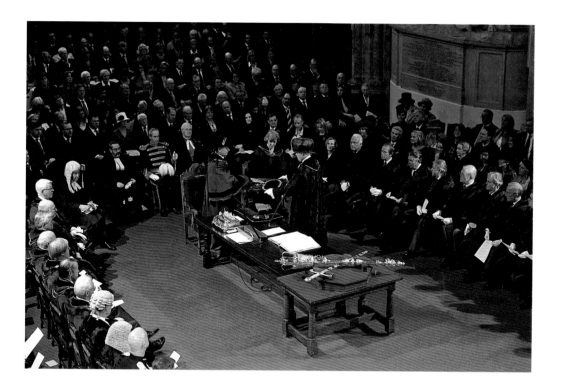

Edward III, who had defaulted on repayments. On 10 March 1415 Henry told the Mayor and Aldermen of London at the Tower that he intended to reconquer the possessions of the Crown in France and that he needed money. Four days later the Archbishop of Canterbury, the Bishop of Winchester and the King's youngest brothers, John, Duke of Bedford and Humphrey, Duke of Gloucester, met the City dignitaries at Guildhall. On 16 June 1415 the City offered a loan of 10,000 marks to the King, receiving a golden collar as security. Henry personally wrote to other cities and to wealthy individuals to ask for money for his campaign in France, which was "for the common good of his beloved subjects". Loans (without interest, as usury was forbidden by the Church) were made by a number of individuals countrywide, including John Hinde, a liveryman of the Worshipful Company of Mercers in the City, who made the single largest personal loan, and Richard Whittington.

Whittington later lived in Hart Street, having become extremely wealthy through the cloth trade, and the story goes that he entertained Henry V there at a sumptuous dinner and threw into the fire all the bonds for the money the King owed him, prompting Henry's thankful exclamation, 'Had ever a King such a subject?' and Whittington's courtly response, 'Had ever a subject such a King?'

The Silent Ceremony held at Guildhall has not changed significantly in over 800 years. The inkstand can be seen on the table, and the City Sword and Mace in the foreground. The outgoing Lord Mayor, Fiona Woolf, next to the incoming Lord Mayor, Alan Yarrow, is touching the Chain of Office, carried on a cushion by the Swordbearer.

21

News of the victory at Agincourt on 25 October 1415 took four days to reach London, just as Henry V arrived at Calais. It was proclaimed in St Paul's Cathedral, bells of the City churches were rung and *Te Deums* sung. That same day, 29 October, was when the newly elected Mayor was to ride to Westminster Palace to be sworn in formally to his office. When he heard the good news, Nicholas Wotton, the new Mayor, decided to break with precedent, and he, the aldermen and an "immense number of the commonalty of the citizens of the city" went "like pilgrims on foot" to Westminster Abbey.

The victorious Henry V arrived in Dover on 16 November, to be greeted by a flamboyant pageant. On 23 November he was met at Blackheath by the Mayor and aldermen, dressed in scarlet gowns, who had ridden out from the City to meet him. They rode to Southwark and then to the City over London Bridge. The City was decorated everywhere with the royal coat of arms and standard, and trumpets played and choirs sang along the royal route. One song, the only one in English which directly addressed the King, started "Welcome Henry ye fifte, Kynge of Englond and of Fraunce", and may have been the famous 'Agincourt Carol'. Henry was showered with valuable gifts of gold by the City, and the celebrations ended with a service at St Paul's Cathedral.

Given this background, the story of the City's role in the Battle of Agincourt, we understand how the Crystal Sceptre came to be given to the City by King Henry V.

To place all this in context, the other regalia of the Lord Mayor and the most significant items of the gold and silver collection will also be described and their stories told.

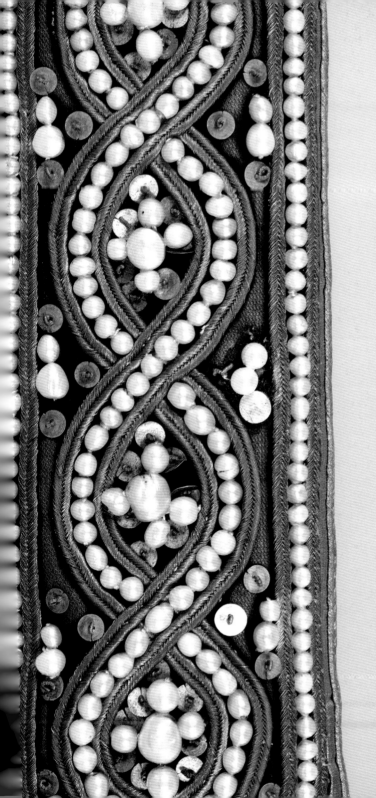

THE MANSION
HOUSE PLATE
COLLECTION

1

The Crystal Sceptre

Paris and London, c. 1380 and c. 1420
Rock-crystal, gold, sapphires, spinels, pearls and painted vellum, 43.2 cm long
Presented by King Henry V to the City, c. 1420–21

This sceptre, or mace, is the most ancient and honourable item of the City regalia. Used at the Silent Ceremony – held at the Guildhall on the Friday before the second Saturday in November, when the outgoing Lord Mayor passes his authority to the incoming – it is also carried by the Lord Mayor at coronations. Though it is a composite object, it can be dated with some accuracy – with elements made at two dates in the late fourteenth and early fifteenth centuries. It is first recorded as being carried by the Lord Mayor at the coronation of Queen Catherine of Valois, wife of Henry V, on 23 February 1421.

It is composed of two tapering rods of rock-crystal, carved with triple spiral flutes set in similarly fluted bands of gold with two bosses of carved crystal at one end and in the middle. The central facetted boss is a nineteenth-century glass replacement. Bands of drilled pearls separate each element. The flared head of the sceptre is set with an earlier, probably French, votive crown of gold, with four cross-pattées and four fleurs-de-lis set with pearls and eight sapphires and spinels. The sapphires, pale blue in colour, are Sinhalese, while the spinels, or balas rubies, are from Central Asia. One sapphire has been drilled and a spinel is badly chipped. The interior of the crown is set with a vellum disc painted with the royal arms of England first used by Henry V after 1406. The artist can be identified as working for the King's brother Humphrey, Duke of Gloucester later in the century. Its great age is revealed by several obvious and rather clumsy repairs to the crown and to the flared head, which has split in places.

The City provided great support to Henry V during the French campaigns that culminated in the Battle of Agincourt in 1415 (see Introduction, pp. 20–22). That a magnificent sceptre, set with a crown and the royal arms, should be provided to the City at this important moment after an historic victory by the sovereign is entirely fitting. The sceptre compares very favourably with other treasury objects of the period, rare survivals and unique in England. The 'Crown of Blanche of Lancaster' made in Paris c. 1370–80 (now in Munich) for Anne of Bohemia, first wife of Richard II, is the closest in technique and design to the crown of the Crystal Sceptre. The spiral fluting of the crystal rods is closely comparable in form to the tusk of narwhal, thought in the Middle Ages to be a unicorn horn and imbued with magical properties. Parisian craftsmen almost certainly made the crown, taken from an image of the Virgin, and carved the crystal, and the whole was probably put together in London and the royal arms painted by an Englishman, identified as working in a scriptorium in St Paul's Churchyard in the City.

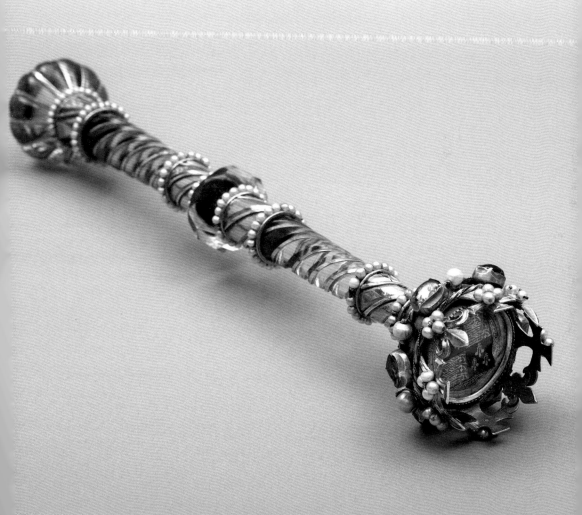

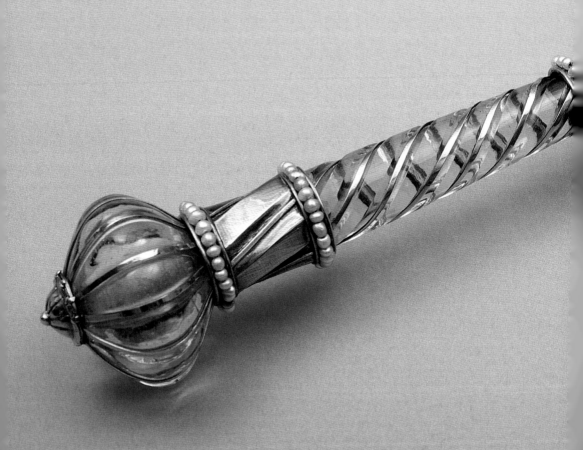

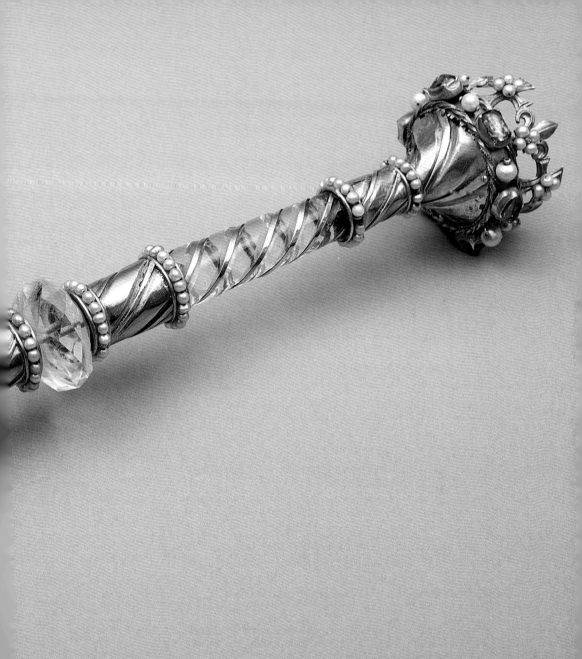

2

The Chain of Esses

Possibly by Robert Adamas, London, c. 1530–35, with later additions and alterations
Gold and enamel, 765 gm
Bequeathed by Sir John Allen (LM 1525–26 and 1535–36) to the City in 1544

Made of cast and chased gold decorated with enamel, the chain has a central link in the form of a portcullis, from which two chains are attached at the upper corners, falling on either side. A ring at the bottom allows the Lord Mayor's Badge (no. 3) to be attached. Eleven enamelled Tudor roses – the red Lancastrian and white Yorkist five-petalled roses conjoined – are backed by five green enamel sepals and are flanked by gold esses, 22 in all. Each group is separated by ten gold double knots, making 44 links. The roses are counter-enamelled fairly crudely on the reverse and the central gold pistil is cast separately and attached through the enamelled flowers by simple gold flanges turned out against the counter-enamel.

The Tudor iconography of the chain is entirely congruent with its date. The portcullis, the badge of the Beaufort family, is a reminder of Henry VII's claim to the throne through his mother, Lady Margaret Beaufort. The conjoined roses recognize the claims of York and Lancaster, united by Henry VII, while the double knot was a popular medieval device representing friendship and loyalty. The origin of the symbolism of the letter S, from which the chain derives its name, is obscure: fifteenth-century chivalric literature attributes to the letter *sanctedat*, *saviensa*, *sapienca* and *seynoria* – sanctity, wisdom, learning and lordship – while Queen Philippa of Hainault hung her chamber with fabric woven with 'S' to represent *souverayne*, sovereignty, a motto also adopted by Henry IV. The double S may also refer to the *Spiritus Sanctus*, the Holy Spirit, though the extant Tudor examples and representations of similar chains often show single letters, as in the present case.

The chain is frequently referred to as 'the Thomas More' chain, and Thomas More does indeed wear a similar chain in the portrait of him by Holbein in the Frick Collection, New York. Despite numerous anecdotes to the contrary, there is nothing to link the Lord Mayor's chain to More. Its history is actually very clear. It was bequeathed to the City by a former Lord Mayor, Sir John Allen (LM 1525–26 and 1535–36), in his will, dated 3 August 1544, which asked that it be held in his chantry chapel next to the Hospital of St Thomas of Acon and the Mercer's Hall, his livery company, and brought to the Lord Mayor when required – a request quickly ignored. A member of the Henry VIII's Privy Council, Allen helped calm the City during the Pilgrimage of Grace, working closely with Thomas Cromwell, and he reluctantly accepted a second term as Lord Mayor at the king's request. He was present at the trial and execution of Anne Boleyn. A chain of esses from the hand of the king was his reward. Robert Adamas – well recorded as a goldsmith who worked

REPLICAS

The Travelling Chain
Hinklenton & Phillips,
London, 1961–62
Silver-gilt and enamel

Toye, Kenning & Spencer,
London, 1981–82
Gold and enamel
Presented by Sir Edward
Howard (LM 1971–72), Col.
the Lord Mais (LM 1972–73),
Sir Murray Fox (LM 1974–75),
Sir Robin Gillett (LM 1976–
77) and Sir Peter Gadsden
(LM 1979–80) in 1981

extensively for Henry VIII and Cardinal Wolsey, providing valuable gold cups and other objects as gifts from the Crown – has been suggested as the maker of this chain. He died in 1534 so it may have been supplied by 1530, before Allen's second term. The uniformity of the design of the heavier links of knots and esses tend to indicate that they were slush-cast from a single mould then chased, while the roses are raised from thin sheets of gold, enamelled in three colours and then assembled. Damaged areas reveal that the gold has been scored to allow the enamel to hold.

The chain has led a wearisome life, being in constant use for over 480 years. It was quickly regarded as too short, so in 1567 it was enlarged with four esses, two knots and two roses at a cost of £23 19s 10d: "yt ys somewhat to short and not so comely to be worn as yt will be then". It is not possible to distinguish which links were then added. Kept at the Guildhall until at least the late eighteenth century, it survived the Great Fire of 1666 but it is not recorded how or by whom. It has been constantly repaired, as the enamel in particular is very fragile. The thin links joining the elements together show much evidence of soldering, not always of the best workmanship. It was repaired seven times between 1716 and 1746 alone, when it was finally provided with a case. In 1895 it was reported that it comprised twelve roses and that "at least one of the roses was quite modern, replacing one that was lost". This modern replacement was subsequently removed. Though still in use on high days and holidays the chain is nowadays often substituted by two replicas, which relieve the burden of everyday wear and tear.

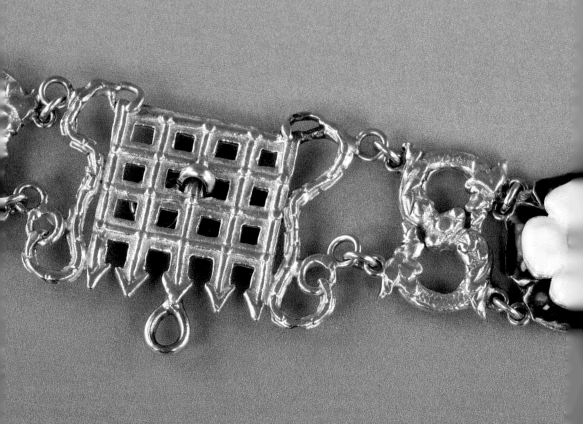

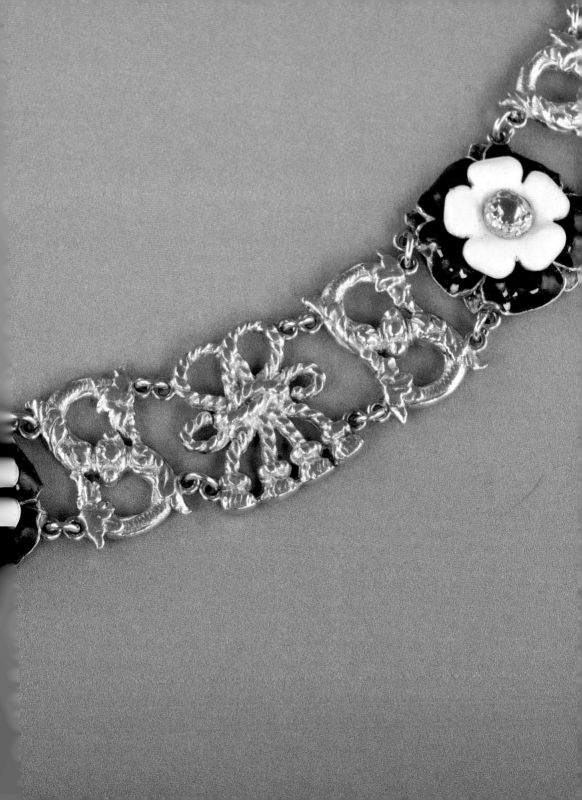

3
The Lord Mayor's Badge

Rundell, Bridge & Rundell, London, 1802–03, and older material
Gold, enamel, onyx and diamonds, 9.8 cm long, 190 gm

In 1558 Sir Martin Bowes (LM 1545–46) gave the City a gold cross set with pearls and precious stones, to be hung from the Chain of Esses. Suspended beneath was a large pear-shaped pearl, purchased by the City for £8 in 1572. This jewel lasted until 1607, when a new one was bought for £480, a considerable sum. It retained the old cross as "a rememberance of him who gave it", and new and old jewels along with the chain were given up to the Chamberlain for safe-keeping at the Guildhall. The old cross has since disappeared. Remade again in 1704, the new jewel, often recorded in portraits of Lord Mayors, was heavily set with diamonds, some 132 when first made, and retained the pendant pearl. The diamonds may well have been recut and re-used in 1802–03, when the present badge was first fashioned by the royal goldsmiths Rundell, Bridge & Rundell and set with an onyx cameo carved with the full arms of the City. The portrait of Sir Christopher Clitherow (LM 1635–36) in the Guildhall collection shows the old badge very clearly, with table-cut diamonds in a broadly lozenge-shaped jewel and the pearl. Still on the 1706 jewel when Joseph Highmore painted the portrait of Sir John Barnard (LM 1737–38), the pearl was missing when Harvey Coombe (LM 1798–99) was painted in 1799. Its loss might have occasioned the jewel being sent to Rundells to recut the diamonds and remake it into its present form.

The Rundell badge originally had eight roses alternating with esses round the cameo, but in 1867 it was again altered, dispensing with the esses to include shamrocks and thistles with the roses, and a blue enamel garter surround with the City motto Domine dirige nos (Lord guide us) set in tiny rose diamonds. Though it is impossible to identify the artist of the cameo, the immense interest in gem-carving in the late eighteenth century brought a number of notable craftsmen to prominence, including the Edward Burchs, father and son, and the brothers William and Charles Brown, who were all carving intaglios and cameos in London at this date. Further diamonds enhance the loop with which the Badge is suspended from the Chain of Esses, or from a blue ribbon for less formal use. The settings for the diamonds were again replaced in 1969. The back, a solid gold oval plate, is also engraved with the City arms and motto, Domine dirige nos. Like the Chain of Esses and the Mace, the Badge has less valuable friends to take its place on occasions or when the Lord Mayor travels.

REPLICAS

The Travelling Badge
Asprey & Co., London,
1975–76
Gold, enamel, onyx and
synthetic stones

Duplicate
Unknown maker and date
Gilt metal and paste

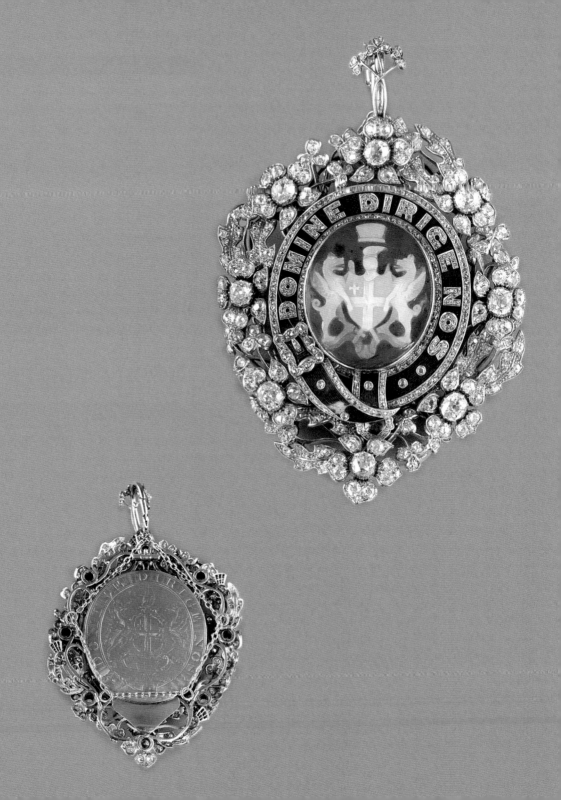

4

The Pearl Sword

HILT Maker unknown, possibly London, c. 1570; silver-gilt
SCABBARD Maker unknown, London, c. 1580–1600; silver-gilt, pearls, velvet
BLADE Maker unknown, Passau, Germany, c. 1560; damascened steel, 160.8 cm long

Behind the City coat of arms a sword is crossed with a mace, representing the two forms of
authority granted by the sovereign and Parliament to the Lord Mayor and Corporation. In
official ceremonies the Mace (no. 7) is borne by the Sergeant-at-Arms and a sword is carried
by the Lord Mayor's Swordbearer – an office certainly extant by 1419. Originally the sword
was the Lord Mayor's personal property, or given by his livery company. It was not until the
early sixteenth century that the City acquired its own weapon, along with the fur Cap of
Maintenance for the Swordbearer, which has the key to Christ's Hospital and City Seals in its
lining. After the Silent Ceremony the Swordbearer gives the key to the outgoing Lord Mayor,
who gives it to the new Lord Mayor, who then gives it back to the Swordbearer, saying "Keep
it under your hat". In 1534 the sword was provided with three scabbards for different uses
– of 'tissue' (that is, cloth of gold) for State occasions, of crimson velvet for ordinary use, and
of black velvet for times of mourning. These functions are now fulfilled by three different
swords, and the Pearl Sword is carried by the Lord Mayor himself before the Sovereign on
State occasions.

The Pearl Sword's history is unclear. Records show that four fine swords came to the City
in the sixteenth century. After the sword with three scabbards came the gift of Sir Ralph
Warren in 1545 (LM 1536–37 and 1544–45), described as "a yerye goodly sworde & a ryche
scaberd of crymsyn velvett". A sword with a silver-gilt pommel, hilt and chape was bought
by the City in 1554, and in 1563 Richard Matthew, a citizen and Cutler, gave a "goodly
sword well and workmanly wrought and gylded". Tradition tells that Queen Elizabeth I
gave the present sword to the City in January 1571, when she opened the newly built Royal
Exchange of her great friend Sir Thomas Gresham. Stylistically it is closest in date to 1570.

The pommel, quillons and chape are silver-gilt, cast and chased, with a figure of Justice –
blindfolded and carrying a sword and scales – on either side of the pommel, which also has
a separate peen covering the end of the tang, which allows the blade to be removed from
the hilt. The quillons and quillon block are elaborately Mannerist in style, with trophies on
either side and figures of satyrs reclining under the extended ends. The first mount above
the quillon block, which has a release for the scabbard, bears the City arms and shows that
it was made to be carried upright. It is also of a different colour of gold and of different
workmanship to the hilt, possibly indicating an addition to an existing sword. The chape is
decorated with the figure of Minerva and a female warrior. The steel blade has been blued
with trophies, acanthus and the City arms. The scabbard of crimson velvet and gold gimp is
sewn with over 2,600 small, mostly Oriental pearls, and some larger pearls of good quality.

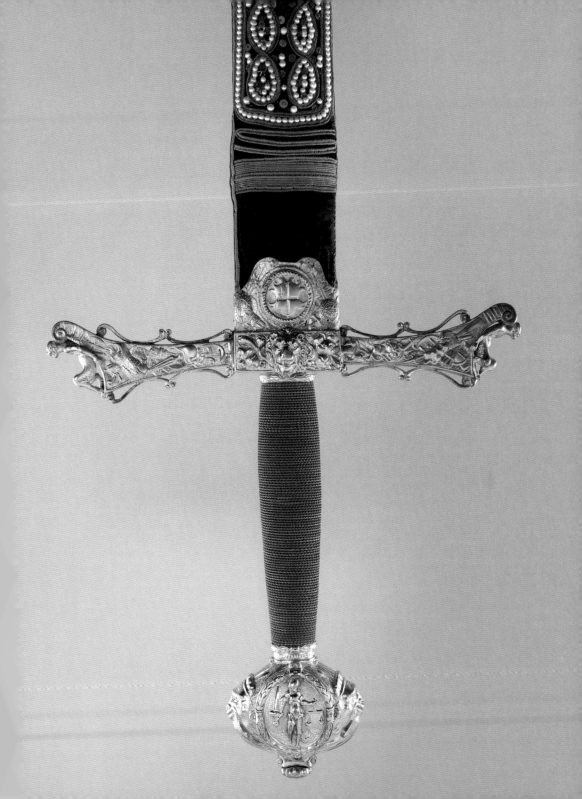

5

The State Sword

SCABBARD Unknown maker, London, 1680–81; silver-gilt, enamel and velvet, 130 cm long
BLADE Italy or Germany, incused, 16th century?; damascened steel
Made for Sir Patrick Ward (LM 1680–81)

The date of 1680–81, when the blade and hilt were joined, can be confirmed by the iconography of the quillon terminals. Often described as lion heads, they are actually those of camels, supporters from the arms of the Merchant Taylors' Company, the livery of Sir Patience Ward, Lord Mayor in that year. The blade has a single, wide groove, stamped FERARA on one side and ZANDONA on the other, along with the running-wolf mark of Passau. It has been engraved and damascened in gold. Despite its length it has no ricasso, which might indicate that it has been cut, but it has never been removed from the hilt for examination. The name 'Ferara' is attached to a large number of swords from the sixteenth to the eigheenth century. Two brothers, Giovani Donato and Andrea de Ferrara, from Belluno in Friuli, were well known as swordmakers by 1580. A very large number of their blades are to be found in Scotland, and many Scottish broadswords or claymores of the early seventeenth century have blades with a distinctive broad central groove that are signed by Andrea Ferrara. Such swords found their way in great quantity into England during the Civil War, and one is shown in the hands of Oliver Cromwell in the 1651 engraved frontispiece of Hobbes's *Leviathan*. The addition on the State Sword of the Passau mark and the second unrecorded name, however, makes its blade impossible to identify.

The silver-gilt pommel, quillons, quillon block and the six lockets of the scabbard were all made by the same unknown maker, the block and the first locket bearing the City arms on one side and on the other royal arms - those of the House of Stuart, commensurate with the late seventeenth-century date. The five further lockets are of cherubs' heads with wings, alternating with two silver-gilt and enamel City arms, a crowned rose, a crowned thistle and the royal arms of 1816–30, giving a date for their addition, along with the damascened royal arms on the blade. From the direction of the figures of Justice on the pommel and the arms on the hilt, it is clear that the sword was made to be carried upright before the Lord Mayor in procession, though the lockets are in the correct direction when carried point down in the presence of royal representatives at the Law Courts or Parliament. Borne before the Lord Mayor by his Swordbearer at civic events, it has, like the other main pieces of regalia, a modern understudy.

An ardent Protestant, Sir Patience, MP for Pontefract, was a founder of what became the Whig party and went into exile for five years for his opposition to Charles II and James II. Ward's unusual first name was the result of his father's vow after having six sons to name his next child Patience, regardless of the gender. He was true to his word.

REPILICA

Wilkinson Sword Ltd,
London, 1963–64
Silver-gilt, steel and velvet,
135 cm
Presented by Sir Ralph
Perring (LM 1962–63)

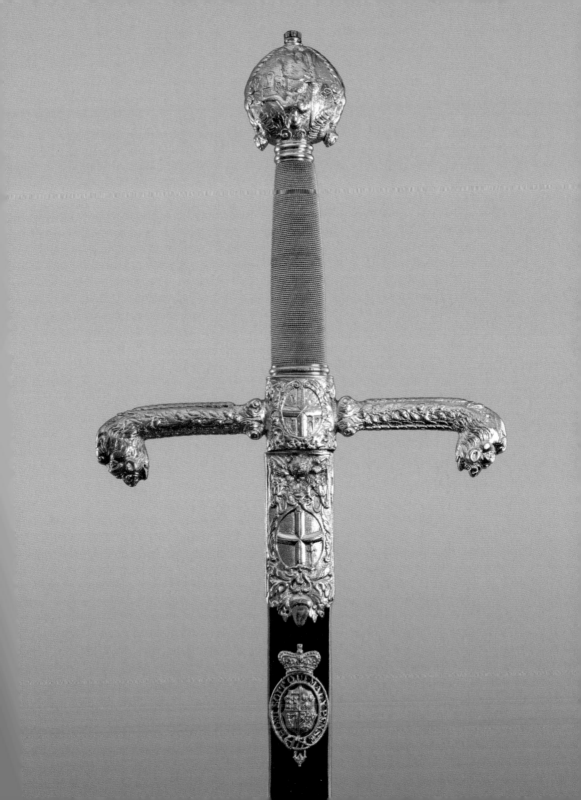

6

The Mourning Sword

Makers unknown, probably German or Hungarian, 16th century?
Steel, 128.3 cm long

Although formerly this sword was borne before the Lord Mayor on Good Friday, all Fast
Days and the anniversary of the Great Fire, it is now only seen at State Funerals, the most
recent of those being Sir Winston Churchill in 1965 and Baroness Thatcher in 2013. The
ancient blade, probably German or Hungarian, and sixteenth-century, has a black enamel
hilt (recently painted) and a scabbard newly covered in black velvetine, all unadorned.
The blade bears three sets of armourers' markings in the form of dots, crescents and
stars, which, though they cannot be identified, are also found on blades in the Wallace
Collection, the Tower of London and in public collections in Berlin, Paris and St Petersburg.
It is believed on no written evidence that the blade was uncovered in the mud of the
Thames in the sixteenth century and presented to the Lord Mayor. Certainly, as early
as 1534 a black sword was provided to the Swordbearer, along with a black damask and
velvet-trimmed robe. The hilt and scabbard are most likely nineteenth-century in origin.

The sword has been stuck in its scabbard for some time, and in 2013 it underwent
x-rays and a CT scan at the Portland Hospital, which confirmed that the blade is likely
to be sixteenth century in origin.

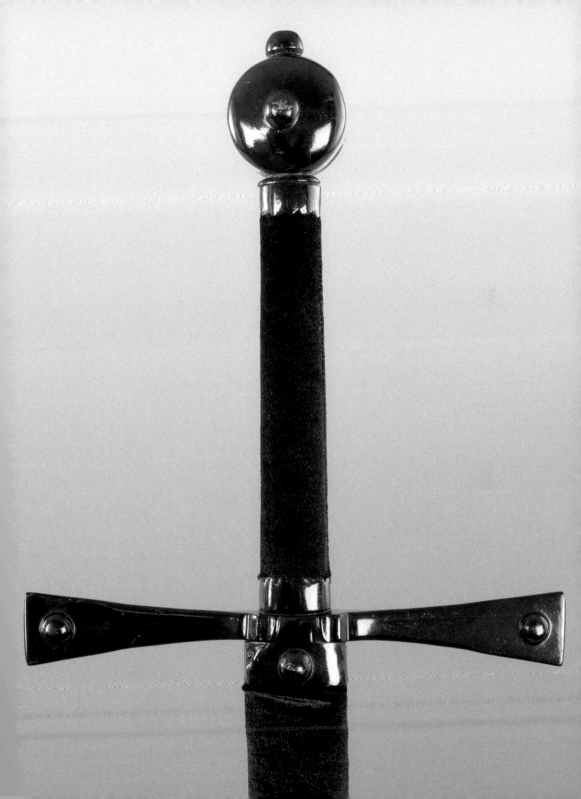

7
The Mace

John White, London, 1735–36
Silver-gilt, 160 cm long, 9,455 gm
Commissioned by the Court of Aldermen in 1734

In 1649, in conformity with the Parliamentary order that all maces in England should be remade in the same form and pattern as that of the House of Commons, the City acquired a new mace at a cost of £81 13s from Thomas Maunday, the maker of Parliament's prototype. Echoes of the earliest extant mace design, the City's own Crystal Sceptre, are seen in the wide head or rompe, surrounded by a crown which contains the royal arms, reflecting the authority granted by the sovereign to the highest representative of the City, the Lord Mayor. Though the Crystal Sceptre is the first and ultimate mace of the City, a mace to be borne by the Sergeant-at-Arms before the Lord Mayor had existed since at least the sixteenth century. This mace was repeatedly remade and repaired over the centuries, as the records show – in 1559, 1600 and 1604 (when it was stolen), and in 1627 and 1649. At the Restoration yet another new mace was ordered, from the former Lord Mayor and Goldsmith Sir Thomas Vyner (LM 1653–54). Again repaired and 'new washed', or re-gilded, regularly, it was finally replaced in 1734, when the Court of Aldermen commissioned the present mace.

Made at a cost of £229 17s 6d by John White, it was still in the manner of the Parliamentary original of 1649. He was allowed £76 8s for the bullion value of the old mace, but £10 3d was deducted from the cost for over-charging. White, from Wareham in Dorset, died in 1789. He produced high-quality work and was either a skilled engraver himself or employed someone who was. As the form of the Mace was well established, it is only in the execution that he was able to display his talents – for casting, heavily raised work, engraving and fine finishing in the chasing. Only the royal arms incorporating those of Hanover with the initials of George II differentiate it significantly from earlier models. The four compartments of the rompe, cast in sections and hollow, are separated by bands of pateræ and contain a rose and thistle, a fleur-de-lis and harp, the King's initials and the City arms. The marks are elegantly spread about on all the separate sections.

The mace is inscribed in various places with the name of the Lord Mayor at its making – Sir Edward Bellamy (LM 1734–35) – and the names of the Lord Mayors and Sergeants-at-Arms at the dates of repair and re-gilding. Wear is most obvious on the central section, where it is handled often, so it obtained a friend in the 1960s to relieve the burden of work.

REPLICA
Wakely & Wheeler, London, 1961–62
Silver-gilt, 165 cm long, 8,647 gm
Presented by Ald. James Harman, 1961 (Sir James Harman, LM 1963–64)

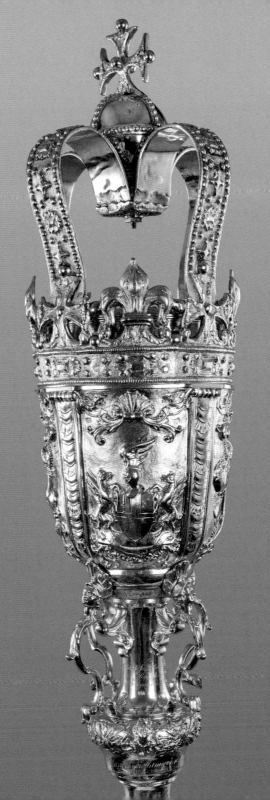

8

The Treloar Badge

Unknown maker, London?, 1906–07
Gold, enamel, shell cameo and diamonds, 5 x 3.8 cm, 36 gm
Made for Lady Treloar, wife of Sir William Treloar (LM 1906–07);
acquired by the City in 2006

This replica of the Lord Mayor's Badge (no. 3) is set with diamonds and a shell cameo replica of the City arms. The garter with the City motto is in plain gold and enamel, rather than bordered in diamonds as it is in the original. A lengthy inscription on the reverse gives details of its early history. Made for Lady Treloar, it was given by Sir William Treloar, after the death of his wife in 1909, to Sir William Dunn (LM 1916–17). Sir William in turn returned it in 1918 to Treloar's adopted daughter Florence, who at some point gave it to the 4th Lord Burnham, Director of the Treloar Trust, set up by Sir William Treloar for the education of disabled children. It was inherited by William Lawson, 5th Baron Burnham, from whom it was bought by Mr Dennis Nicholson for the Merchant Taylors' Company in 1984, so that it might be presented to commemorate the 500th anniversary of the Billesdon Award.

In 1484 Lord Mayor Robert Billesdon had settled the dispute between the Skinners and the Merchant Taylors over their place in the order of company precedence by having them alternate the sixth and seventh places each year. While the Skinners spell the award Billesdon, the Merchant Taylors spell it Billesden. It is now worn by the Lord Mayor's spouse or by Lord Mayors themselves if a lady.

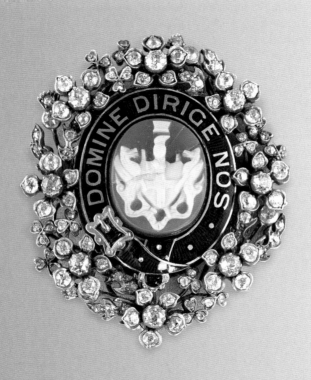

9
The Fire Cup

Maker unknown, WM in a shield above a mullet between two pellets, London, 1662–63
Silver-gilt, 34 cm high, 1112 gm
Made from a cup presented by Robert Christopher, Clothworker,
to the City in 1580; remade three times

This is the only piece of silver at Mansion House to pre-date the Great Fire of London of
1666. It had already been remade three times, the original silver having been presented
to the City by one Robert Christopher, a member of the Clothworkers' Guild in 1580.
Christopher had been Master of the guild in 1562 and a "secondarie to the Comptors", or
deputy to one of the two Sheriffs, and this piece was a bequest to the City, as an inscription
around the rim records. Of a standard seventeenth-century form, on a tall baluster foot,
the bowl was probably made to unscrew to allow it to be stored and carried. Part of the
ceremonial plate of great households and wealthy liveries, cups of this sort were for display
as well as toasts. It is almost identical to the Pack Cup of the Drapers' Company, dated 1682,
which shows how taste and style changed very little over twenty years. The band of matt
ground round the body has two reserves, one blank and the second engraved with the City
arms, but very simply done without the usual 'tricking', allowing the colours of the arms
to be read – in this case a red cross and red sword on a silver ground. The finial of the lid
is cast. Christopher's original "bolle with a cover of silver all guylte" weighed 1219 gm, a
good deal more than its replacement, a diminution probably accounted for by the cost of
refashioning.

Many of the livery companies lost their treasure in the Great Fire, particularly those
whose halls lay close to the source in Pudding Lane, the Dyers and Watermen being the
first to be burnt on day one. The Mercers' plate was melted, with 200 lb of silver salvaged
afterwards, while the Drapers' silver was mostly saved by the Renter Warden, who threw
it into a sewer, forgetting only a hoard of coin, 446 lb in weight, which melted but was
recovered as a lump. Sir Thomas Bludworth, Lord Mayor at the time of the fire, was feeble
in the extreme in fighting the blaze, but was nevertheless extremely able to save his own
property from his magnificent mansion in Aldersgate. Behind St Paul's Cathedral, it
only burnt on the third day of the fire, allowing Sir Thomas time to remove his treasure,
including the City plate, to safety. He, too, apparently suffered losses, however: his will,
dated 24 November 1680, mentioned that it had "pleas'd God to lessen me in my Estate by
that dreadfull fire of London".

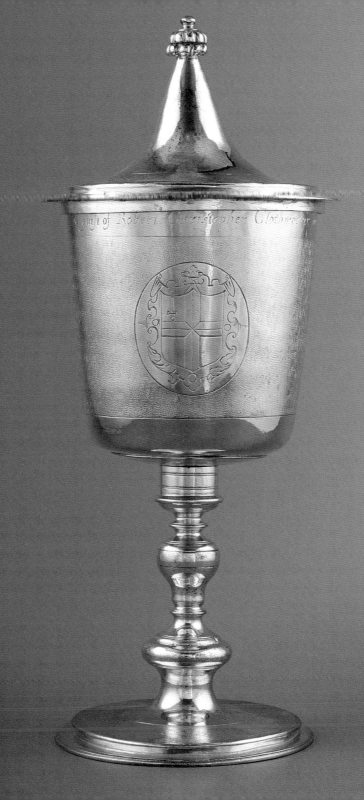

10

A monteith

William Lukin, London, 1699–1700
Silver, Britannia standard, 42.5 cm in diameter, 30 cm high, 5482 gm
Probably presented by William Dormer, Swordbearer to the City in 1741

This hefty fluted bowl with a richly scalloped top edge has cast and chased lion heads with drop-ring handles at either side. The attached rim is cast and chased with winged cherub heads, gadrooned scrolls and embossed foliage. The form of the bowl itself, here raised from a single sheet of silver, would eventually develop to have a detachable rim so that it could serve as either a punch bowl or a monteith and could allow glasses to be hung between the scallops. A feature of any fashionable seventeenth- or eighteenth-century social gathering, punch – from the Sanskrit word 'pañc', meaning five, revealing its Indian origins – was made with five ingredients. The Oxford antiquarian Anthony à Wood, writing in 1683, noted that "in the summer time came up a vessel or bason notched at the brims to let drinking glasses hang there by the foot so that the body or drinking place might stand in the water to cool them. Such a bason was called a 'Monteigh' from a fantastical Scot called 'Monsieur Monteigh' who at that time or a little before wore the bottoms of his cloake or coate so notched U U U U." Though they were soon fashionable, monteiths such as the present example from before the first decade of the eighteenth century are rare, the earliest known belonging to King's College, Cambridge, of 1684–85, while another of 1685–86 belongs to the Drapers' Company. The maker of the present example, William Lukin, was free of his guild only in July 1699, and this is one of the earliest pieces recorded by him. It is made of Britannia-standard silver, of a higher silver content than sterling, a standard that had been introduced only in 1696 to prevent silversmiths clipping or melting the coinage, but was abandoned in 1720.

The arms of the City are matched by a cartouche with scale and strapwork mantling and embossed with the initials of William Dormer, Swordbearer to the Lord Mayor, added later to commemorate his gift of this piece and the State Salt to the City in 1741. The office of Swordbearer was a lucrative sinecure in the eighteenth century, and Dormer paid £2,500 for the post in December 1741, the year of the gift.

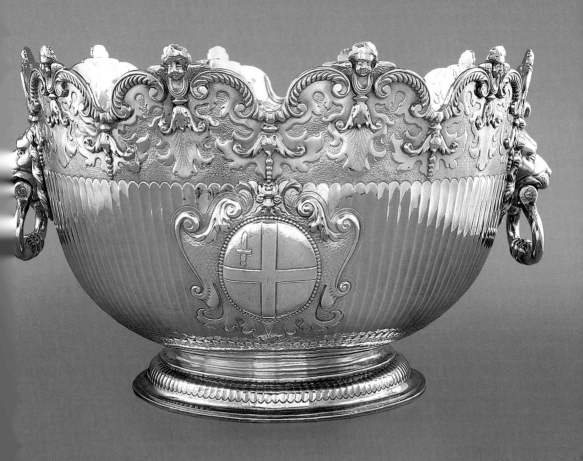

11

A pair of cups and covers, three rosewater dishes, three flagons and three rosewater ewers

Benjamin Pyne, London, 1720–22
Silver-gilt, Britannia standard: cups and covers 45 cm high, 3849 gm gross;
dishes 58.4 cm diameter, 12946 gm gross; ewers 34.2 cm high, 5505 gm gross
Made from pre-Great Fire plate, one dish and ewer replacing those
presented by Dame Margaret North in 1567

Requiring to be refashioned is an occupational hazard of silver in the City. Fortunately
the City has always had access to the greatest workshops and designers, and could call on
the skills of liverymen, Aldermen and even Lord Mayors themselves. From the surviving
indentures – lists and values of the plate handed into the care of every new Lord Mayor –
we can see how taste, use and wear and tear has taken its toll over the centuries. Nearly all
the eighteenth-century plate surviving at Mansion House has an ancestry going back to
the sixteenth or seventeenth centuries. Numerous records of the moments of remaking
survive, with goldsmith Francis Meynell reporting in 1662, for example, that plate was
"out of fashion, battered and unhandsome for service".

A group of useful wares, large in both number and scale, was remade by Benjamin Pyne
in 1721 during the mayorality of Sir John Frayer. Pyne charged £274 10s for the flagons that
he described as "decanters", including the costs of materials, fashioning, engraving, gilding
and three leather cases, against which he deducted £126 1s 9d for re-using older pieces.
The other pieces Pyne made are also fashioned from old plate, sometimes traceable back
to the mid sixteenth century and remade several times – cups and covers, basins and
'trenchers', or salt-cellars, all went into the melting pot in 1721. The choice of Pyne was
a good one. He was an outstanding craftsman, whose work, along with that of Anthony
Nelme, had the simplicity of style and considerable weight in silver so loved during the
reign of Queen Anne.

The differences in colour between the pieces are the result of constant use and regilding,
all recorded in inscriptions. Sometimes these recall an earlier incarnation. Two of the new
pieces, for example, started life as a *fayre bason and ewer of silver algylte*, a gift from Dame
Margaret North in 1567. Widowed four times and childless, Lady North made the Mercers'
Company the residual heir to her large property, and a small part of her donation to the
City is still extant at Mansion House in these pieces. Soon after the set was made, two large
iron-bound chests were provided by Sir George Merttins (LM 1724–25) for plate storage.

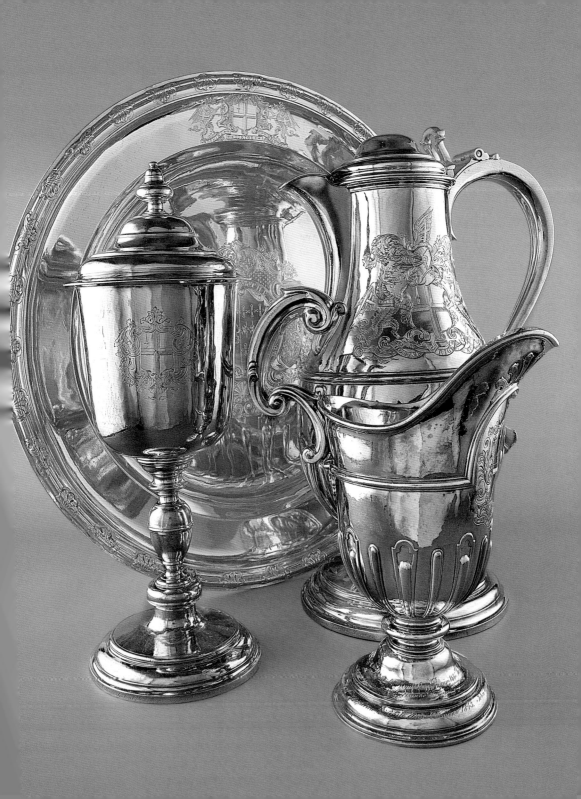

12

The State Salt-cellar

Augustine Courtauld, London, 1730–31
Silver, 24.1 cm high, 2348 gm
Presented by Edward Gestlin, Carver Sergeant, to Thomas Carbonnel, Swordbearer,
in 1731; presented by him to William Dormer, Swordbearer, in 1741, and presented
to the City with a montieth (no. 10) that year

Probably the last of its kind to be made, this form of salt-cellar was already an endangered species by the end of the seventeenth century. Reflecting the social, financial and culinary significance of salt – a commodity with its own livery company that ranks ninth amongst the Great Twelve – salt-cellars had been used to denote wealth and status from the early Middle Ages onwards. The bowl of the present example is cast and decorated with applied strapwork, set on four hollow cast and chased dolphin-shaped legs, which stand on shell feet, all referring to the saline contents. From the rim of the bowl rise four hollow cast and chased scrolled arms ending in children's heads, which, along with the acquatic legs, give a foretaste of the Rococo style. The branches would have supported either a napkin, covering the salt when it was not in use, or a porcelain dish, often of oysters, as seen in depictions of such salts in painted tablescapes. Suffering over the years, probably when the salt-cellar was placed roughly on the table, the dolphin tails have been frequently repaired at the junction with the bowl. To strengthen this delicate junction a thin moulded band of silver has been inserted within the legs, disturbing the aesthetics of the form but stopping it from falling apart.

By the early Georgian period, when salt was plentiful, individual salt-cellars appeared, relegating grandiose centrepieces to ceremonial use and even obsolescence. This salt is not only a fine example of an ancient form, but also a remarkably imaginative and distinguished work of a leading Huguenot silversmith, Augustine Courtauld. Arriving in London in the early 1680s, Courtauld was apprenticed to another exiled Frenchman, Nicolas Pantin. Solid, slightly unimaginative but superbly made work brought him considerable success, though never to the degree of his fellow Huguenot and almost exact contemporary Paul de Lamerie. This salt is generally agreed to be Courtauld's masterpiece.

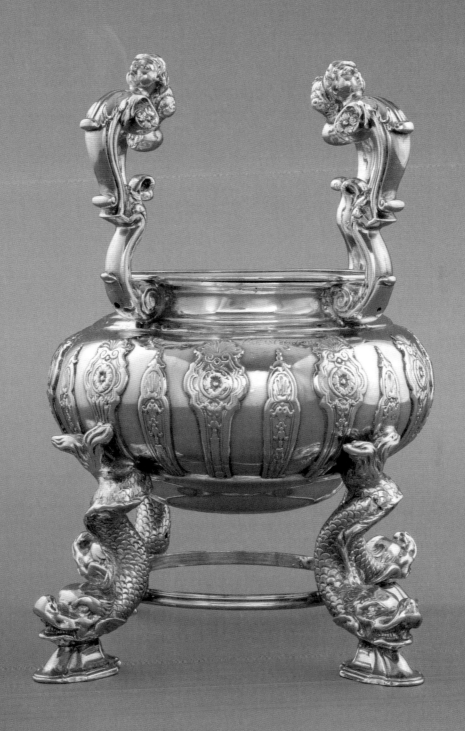

13

Three tankards

Samuel Jeffreys, London, 1731–32
Silver, gilt interior, one 22.8 cm high, 1648 gm; two 17.7 cm, 1135 gm gross
From a silver bowl presented by Sir Bevis Bulmer in 1594

The Fire Cup (no. 9) is all that remains of the City's pre-Fire silver, though these tankards
and a rosewater ewer and bason of 1720–21 (no. 11) are made from earlier silver reworked.
In 1594 the courtier, entrepreneur and mining magnate Sir Bevis Bulmer presented the City
with a silver bowl, weighing some 3714 gm. It commemorated the building of a riverside
horse-driven chain-pump at Broken Wharf near St Paul's to bring water to Cheapside.
The bowl was made from silver mined at Combe Martin in north Devon, a lead-rich seam
that had been mined for silver since the thirteenth century, and which Sir Bevis began
exploiting in 1587. Henry V was able to provide finance for his wars in France that included
his great victory at Agincourt in 1415 from silver mined at Combe Martin – and some of
these coins are extant. The bowl was engraved with a verse:

> When waterworks in Broaken Wharf
> At first erected weare
> And Bevis Bulmer with his art
> The waters 'gan to reare.

Bulmer had started his life of mining operations in Ireland and the lowlands of Scotland
and then mined for tin in Cornwall, while along the way taking out patents for a new form
of lighthouse and a machine that made nails. He then prospected for gold in Scotland,
presenting a porringer made from his finds to Queen Elizabeth in 1595. He eventually died
in poverty in 1613, having dunned King James I out of £3,000 to finance his adventures.

The Bulmer bowl was remade into small pots or tankards in 1634, which in turn were
exchanged in 1662. In 1674 they were remade as four tankards, exchanged yet again in 1689,
and finally refashioned into the present three tankards in 1731, though their trials were
by no means over; in 1845 spouts were ignominiously added. Spectroscopic analysis of the
silver has shown that elements are of a purity far finer than either sterling or Britannia
standard. Inscriptions on each piece record their original donor.

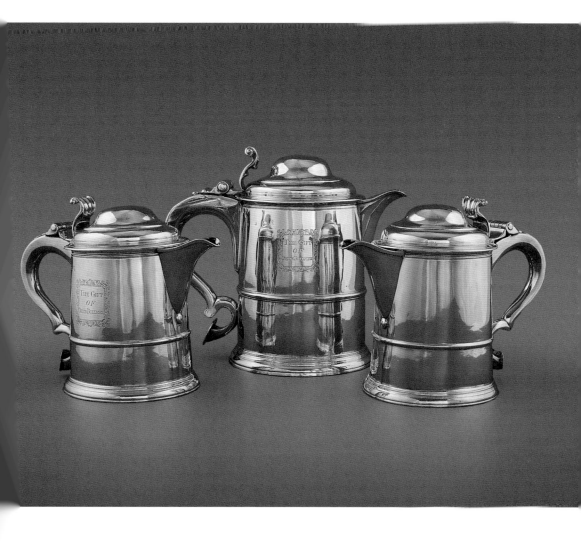

14

Dinner plates, soup plates, meat dishes, a turbot dish, mazarines and associated domes

PLATES 92 Paul de Lamerie, London, 1737–38; two William Cripps, London, 1761–62; one Richard Carter, Daniel Smith & Robert Sharp, London, 1786–87; 24 Paul Storr, London, 1814–15; 24 William Bateman, London, 1818–19: silver, 25.4 cm diameter, 87012 gm gross
SOUP PLATES 24 William Cripps, London, 1761–62; 23 William Grundy, London, 1775–76; one William Grundy, London, 1776–77; twelve William Bateman, London, 1834–35: silver, 25.4 cm diameter, 38965 gm gross
MEAT DISHES ten Paul de Lamerie, London, 1737–38; 2 unmarked, London, 1737–38; four Thomas Gilpin, London, 1748–49; two Paul Storr, London, 1815–16; 20 Paul Storr, London, 1818–19; three William Bateman, London, 1832–33; five Richard Atkins & William Somersall, London, 1833–34; ten William Bateman, London, 1834–35; one Edward Ker Reid, London, 1863–64; one Edward Barnard & Sons, London, 1883–84: silver, various sizes, 46454 gm gross
TURBOT DISH William Bruce, London, 1818–19: silver, 68.5 cm long, 11183 gm gross
MAZARINES 6 William Burwash London, 1815–16: silver, various sizes, 6190 gm gross
(together with one round, eight large and eight small oval domes, plated)

This vast service has served the Lord Mayor and Corporation of London for nearly 300 years. Sir John Barnard was Lord Mayor when the most famous silversmith of the day, Paul de Lamerie, was commissioned to provide the plates, presumably eight dozen, of which most survive, and a dozen meat dishes. The City at the time was wealthy, powerful and prospering, and great changes were in the air. Good with money, Sir John was offered the Chancellorship of the Exchequer by Prime Minister Walpole, but he refused as the salary of £4,000 a year was "inconsiderable". Money raised from the fines he imposed on citizens reluctant to take office, particularly that of Sheriff, meant that a new, permanent home for the Lord Mayor was in the offing. It is said that Mansion House was built for those who wanted to be Lord Mayor out of the pockets of those who did not. Sir John's successor Micajah Perry was to lay the foundation stone for it at Stock's Market in 1739.

A new home needed fine plate for entertaining, and de Lamerie began the service in a spectacular way with plates and serving dishes. The model of a ten-inch circular plate, raised from a single piece of silver, was a common one throughout the eighteenth century. The cast and chased rims of scallops and acanthus were made in sections and applied before the rim was neatly trimmed and finished. In 1814 Paul Storr added two dozen more plates of the same model, an order repeated to William Bateman a few years later, bringing the surviving total of plates to 141, while groups of soup plates, serving dishes, a turbot dish and mazarines - pierced strainers, for roasts and fish, that lay inside the serving pieces - were added over a long period, with the final addition, still to de Lamerie's original design, being made in 1883–84. The service is used today in the Lord Mayor's private dining-room.

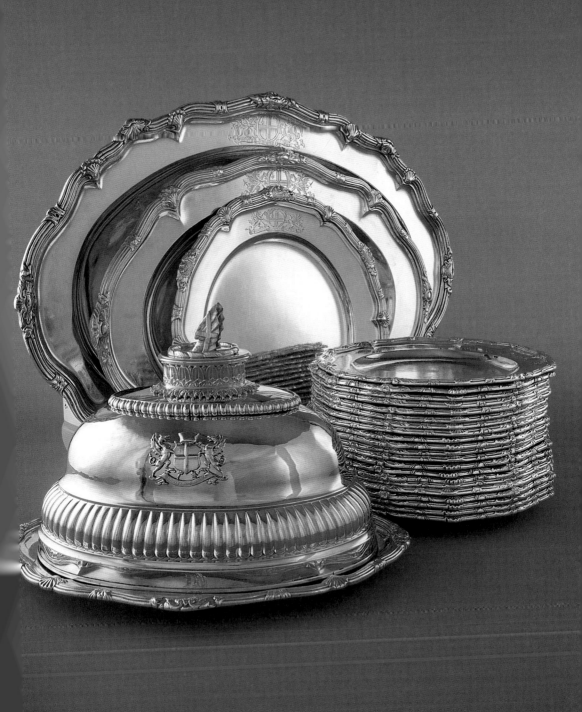

15

An epergne, candelabrum and stand

EPERGNE Paul de Lamerie, London, 1738–39
Silver-gilt, 86 cm long, 81 cm wide, 32 cm high, 11222 gm
CANDLE-HOLDERS AND STAND Paul Storr, London, 1811–12
Silver-gilt, 47 cm long, 40.6 cm wide, 23 cm high, 13025 gm

This elegant epergne of the late 1730s was made by the royal goldsmith Paul de Lamerie in a fluent Rococo style. Sixty years later a bold Neoclassical stand was provided for it by Paul Storr, another royal goldsmith. Not content with that, Storr cut off the rim of the central bowl, extended the bowl downwards, made a basket-weave insertion and put candle-holders and drip-pans at the ends of the eight arms to create an impressive centrepiece at the expense of a fine, if typical, piece of work by London's leading silversmith of the day, which he made in conjunction with the large commission for plates (no. 14).

In its original form the four lower arms would have supported four dishes, three of which survive today. Their former use can be detected by the outlines of the fitments for the arms, now disguised by the engraved arms of the City. The two dishes for the higher arms have disappeared. As these three survivors are plain silver, clearly the epergne was not originally gilded, but the taste and need of the Mayoralty in the early years of the nineteenth century called for grandeur rather than domesticity. The epergne was first altered in 1789 by the then Lord Mayor's own firm of Pickett & Rundell, when the baskets, which are unmarked, were made. William Pickett (LM 1789–90), a practising goldsmith with premises on Ludgate Hill, was originally in partnership with his father-in-law William Theed. He brought his apprentice Philip Rundell into the business in the 1760s, eventually selling 32 Ludgate Hill and his interest to him when Rundell took on John Bridge and a nephew, Edmund Rundell, to create the famous firm of Rundell, Bridge & Rundell, who supplied plate to the City for many years.

Storr worked extensively for and with Rundell in the early years of the nineteenth century. By the time he turned to the epergne its small scale and delicate design would have seemed inadequate for a setting like the Egyptian Hall. It is a testament to Storr's ingenuity that he was able to create such a piece when most silversmiths, confronted with an out-moded epergne, would have been tempted to melt it down and start again. Storr's alterations were based on the premise that with candles the bowl would be too low. His solution of a woven ring to support an enlarged, raised bowl kept the central section light and three-dimensional. With fruit, flowers and candles, the transformation was a success. Epergnes developed from the French practice of allowing guests to serve themselves, and, though French-sounding, they were an English invention of the 1720s onwards.

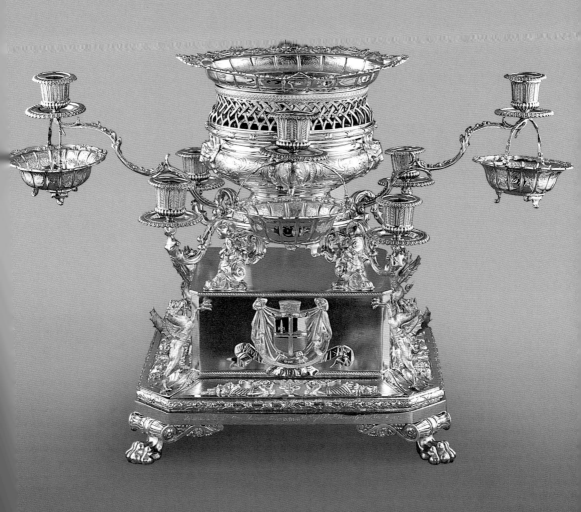

16

The Irish Cup and Salver

Gabriel Sleath, London, 1740–41
Silver-gilt: cup and cover 37 cm high, 3491 gm; salver 40 cm diameter, 1781 gm
Intended for presentation by The Irish Society to Henry Singleton, Lord Chief Justice
of the Common Pleas of Ireland, but refused and presented to the City, 1741

The Honourable The Irish Society was created in the reign of James I as a means to extract
funds from the City and the livery companies by investing in the 'plantation' of northern
Ireland, particularly around the cities of Derry - renamed Londonderry - and Coleraine.
Unfortunately for the monarchy The Irish Society proved to be unbiddable, and, though
the massive immigration of English settlers failed to materialize, investment and
development under the Society's leadership, coupled with an active interest from the
City and the twelve Great livery companies, did much to transform the area.

Support for Irish leadership in Ireland resulted in the creation of this cup, cover and
salver. Henry Singleton, a native of Drogheda and the town's MP for over twenty years,
was a leading lawyer in Ireland. His appointment as Chief Justice of the Common Pleas
of Ireland in 1740 was seen as a victory for the Irish bar at a time when only Englishmen
achieved promotion. To honour this event, The Irish Society commissioned these pieces of
silver to present to him. He refused them, however, and the Society passed them to the City
of London for, as the lengthy inscription on the base of the salver records, *the honour and
grandeur of this City*.

Gabriel Sleath, a skilled and eminent silversmith, was an outspoken critic of the influx
into the London silver trade of Huguenots, who he described as "necissitous strangers",
but he was clearly not above using the latest Rococo styles introduced by them from
France. Though the cup bears the arms of Singleton in one of the cartouches, the other
with the City arms may well have been added when the cup was refused and it came
to Mansion House. It has been extensively repaired and many times re-gilded over the
centuries, each event scrupulously recorded on all three pieces. Re-gilding, which requires
the finer points of the engraving and chasing to be cleared of excess gold, has not helped
the overall appearance.

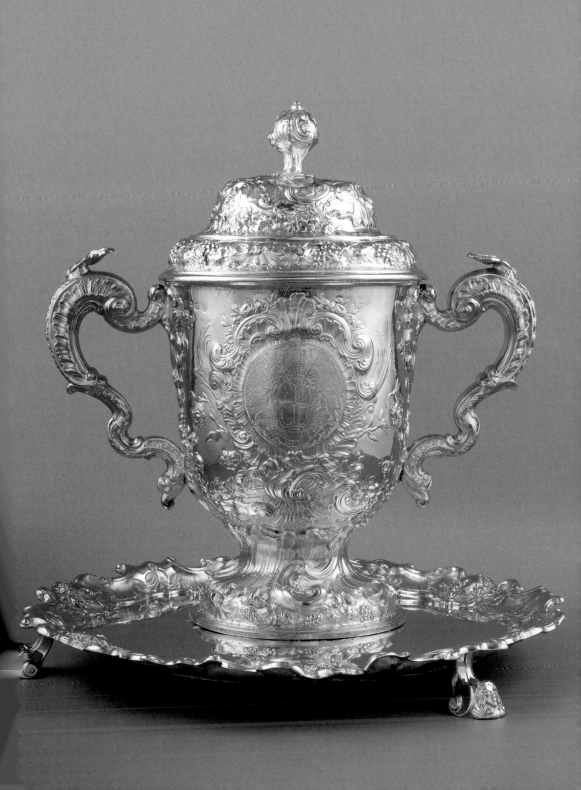

17

Twelve candlesticks and six twin-light branches

William Café, London, 1770–71
Silver, 29.2 cm high, 20054 gm gross
Made in William Beckford's year (LM 1769–70)

This group of candlesticks, along with eight waiters and salvers of various sizes, were provided to the Mansion House during the Mayoralty of one of the most extraordinary Lord Mayors of the eighteenth century – William Beckford. A Jamaican plantation-owner of immense wealth, educated at Westminster School, Balliol College in Oxford and Leiden University in Holland, Beckford lived in the West Indies for many years until he moved to London in 1744, when he entered politics and acquired 5,000 acres at Fonthill, Wiltshire, on which he built a splendid house. It seems contradictory that a vastly wealthy slave-owner should be a radical middle-class government reformer, but his support for William Pitt was unswerving, promoting reforms – for annual Parliaments, equal representation, extension of the franchise, invalidation of general warrants – and championing the rights of the American colonies. He first held the office of Lord Mayor in 1762–63, and returned to Mansion House in 1769. He led a City deputation to the King, protesting at Parliament's overruling of the landslide election of John Wilkes as Member for Middlesex. George III expressed his clear displeasure with Beckford's address, to which the Lord Mayor had the temerity to reply, warning the King of the consequences he faced if he ignored the people. This rebuke earned him respect, affection and, when he died three weeks later of what was described as 'political excitement', a statue in Guildhall.

Though he had a reputation for a violent temper and a streak of vulgarity, his wealth brought these fine candlesticks to Mansion House, where he entertained lavishly during both his Mayoral terms. Horace Walpole described Beckford as a "noisy good humoured flatterer, vulgar and absurd, pompous in his expense, and vainglorious". These cast and chased candlesticks, weighty, tasteful and by the best-known maker of such pieces then living, belie their provenance.

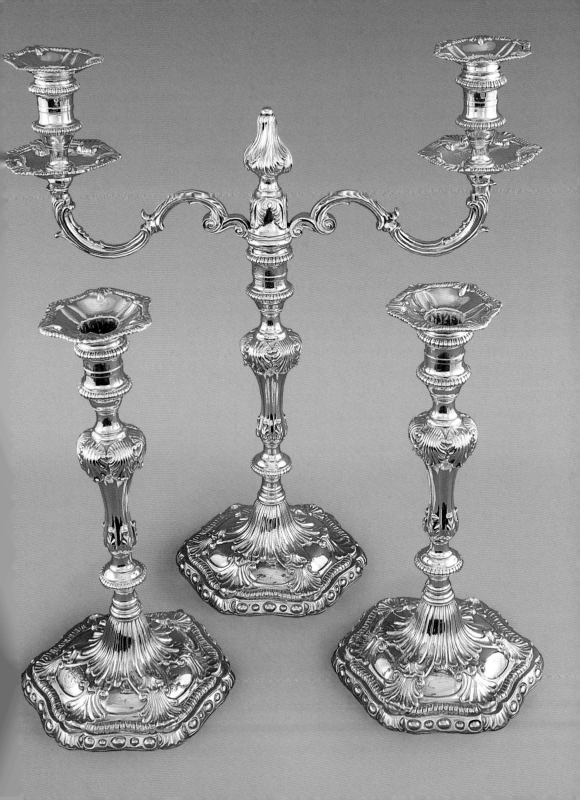

18

The Brass Crosby Cup and Cover

John Romer and George Daniel Gaab, London, 1772–73
Silver, 55.8 cm high, 7541 gm
Presented by Viscount Wakefield (LM 1915–16) in 1935

The most magnificent piece of silver at the Mansion House, this cup has a pleasing and unusual design and is of superb craftsmanship. Also one of the most historic pieces, it commemorates the strengthening of the freedom of the Press in England by the 'Printers' Case' of 1771, when three City MPs – the Lord Mayor Brass Crosby and Aldermen John Wilkes and Richard Oliver – refused to arrest printers in the City who defied the ban on reporting Parliamentary proceedings. The cry of "Wilkes and Liberty!" went up, riots broke out and the leaders of the so-called 'City Patriots' were arrested. When sending Oliver and Crosby to the Tower, the Prime Minister Lord North directed they go by water to avoid their being freed by the irate populus. The City held firm, however, and the men were released, whereupon the Court of Common Council voted for three cups to be made for presentation to the defenders of liberty. The Brass Crosby Cup was to cost £200, while the other two were to cost £100 each (see no. 19).

The round foot of the Crosby Cup, rimmed with berried laurel, stands on a square base cast with a raised meander. The undulating fluting of the stem is decorated with swags of barley husks, a motif that is used to great effect round the two smaller cartouches that contain the arms of Crosby and the City, and those that fall from either side of the handles down the body of the cup. Two satyrs seated on lion-faced brackets form the handles. The satyrs and a kneeling putto on the lid clutch generous bunches of grapes.

The two applied scenes, chased and engraved, are signed by George Daniel Gaab, originally from Augsburg. On one side of the cup is an allegory of the City of London, a seated figure attended by Britannia, Fame, Justice and Liberty, while on the other Crosby is borne home to Mansion House in the State Coach, having been released from the Tower of London, and is surrounded by a jubilant crowd, with a diorama of City monuments behind. The cup was made by another foreign silversmith working in London, John Romer, of Norwegian descent and a friend of Gaab, and it was sold through the firm of Portal & Gearing of Ludgate Hill. Abraham Portal, a failed poet, failed playwright and soon to be failed goldsmith (his newly founded firm went bankrupt in 1778), was a staunch supporter of the King's party and thought Wilkes an interloper in City matters. However, as a close friend of William Nash, who had succeeded Crosby as Lord Mayor in 1772, Portal was given the commission. The allusions to drink in the barley and grapes may well have been Portal's not-so-amusing reference to the terrible gout which delayed Crosby's appearance before the Commons for several days.

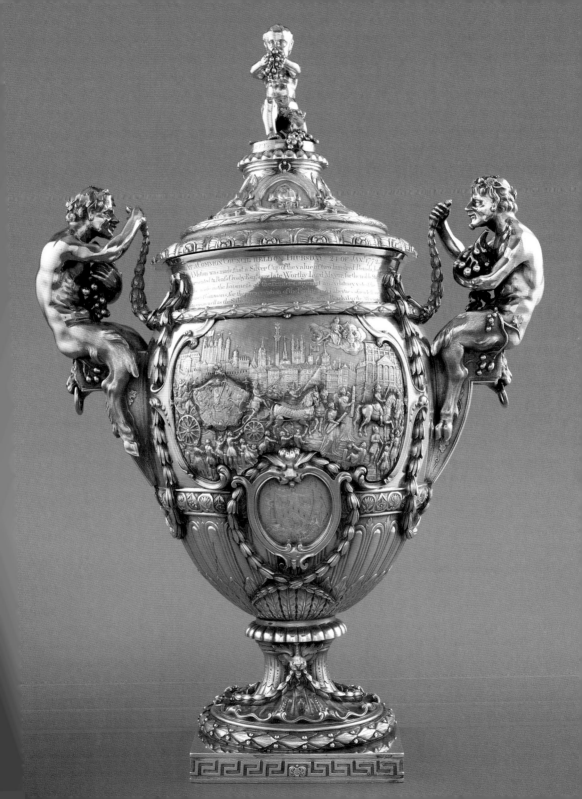

19

The Oliver Cup and Cover

Charles Wright, London, 1772–73
Silver-gilt, 55.8 cm high, 5039 gm
Presented by the City to Alderman Richard Oliver, MP, in 1772
and in turn presented by him to the City

Surmounted by a figure of Liberty, this is the second of the three cups made for
presentation to the defenders of liberty, John Wilkes, Brass Crosby and Richard Oliver.
While this and the Crosby Cup (no. 18) are now at Mansion House, the one presented to
Wilkes has disappeared. Oliver returned his cup to the City to act as a 'publik memorial'
to the events of 1771, as the inscription attests.

   The Neoclassical elements of cast and applied acanthus leaves, fluting, beading and
gadroons contrast with the widely scrolled handles of an earlier period. These elements
show the influence of Robert Adam, who produced some of the earliest Neoclassical designs
for English silver. Adam relied less on antique prototypes than is often assumed, but looked
particularly at Renaissance and Baroque design for inspiration, hence the broadly splayed
handles in auricular curves and the waisted body. It is the old-fashioned work of the
worthy but slightly pedestrian maker Charles Wright, who specialized in the manufacture
of cups and covers. The addition on the handles of dragons, who support the City arms
and gaze proudly up at Liberty, help overcome the slightly awkward overall form. The
allegorical harbour scene engraved on the body reflects Oliver's business as a West India
merchant. Fame and Reason hold up the arms of the City and those of the recipient.
An Alderman for Billingsgate Ward, Oliver was elected MP for the City in 1770, a position
he held for ten years. He eventually fell out with Wilkes, declined the Mayoralty and retired
to his estates in Antigua.

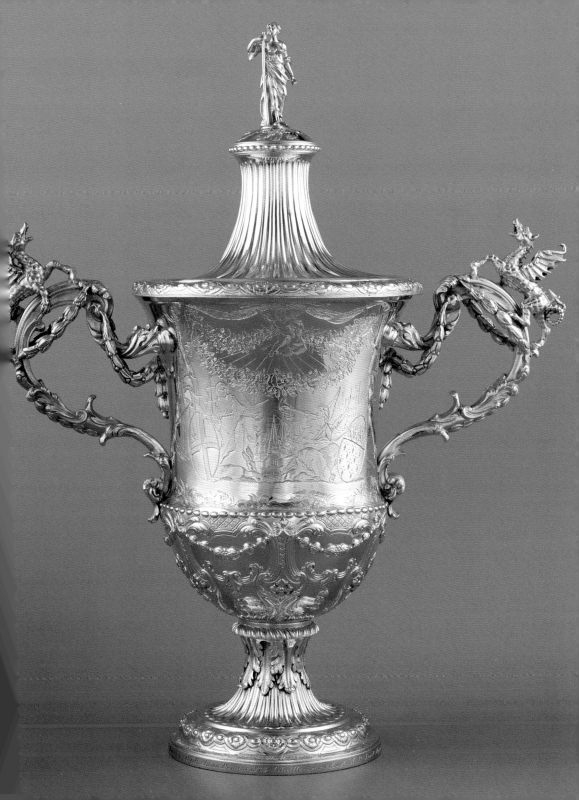

20

The Killik Cup and Cover

Maker's mark WC, London, 1775–76
Silver-gilt, 46 cm high, 4588 gm
Presented by Sir Stephen Killik (LM 1934–35)

This fine, elegant Neoclassical cup and cover, with a raised body, foot and lid, has cast and applied decoration of swags and beading. A well-proportioned piece of this nature was intended to be used purely as decoration on a buffet or sideboard. Based on the prolific designs of Robert Adam of the 1770s, similar cups, tureens and smaller pieces in the newly fashionable urn-shape were produced by London silversmiths for the rest of the century. Dated 1775–76 and marked by WC, the present example has been believed to be by William Cripps. Arthur Grimwade, the *bon-savant* of the history of English silversmiths, however, gives a universally accepted date of 1767 for Cripps's death. There is a register of large-workers missing from the records at Goldsmiths' Hall that covers the period 1758 to 1773. The mark would not have been allowed while Cripps was alive, so it may have been registered after 1767 but before 1775. William Cox, a goldsmith of St Paul's Churchyard, and William Chatterton of Paternoster Row, Spittlefields, are possible contenders, as is William Café, who made the candlesticks at Mansion House (no. 17), but, as he appears to have worked almost exclusively on this form, he should be discounted.

The Mansion House has seven silver-gilt cups and covers from the late eighteenth century that have been presented in the twentieth century by Lord Mayors keen to improve the display of plate. The elegant and impressive large pieces of Georgian silver-gilt were seen as more appropriate gifts than similar pieces of Victorian or contemporary origin. Three are from the 1750s, two from the 1770s and two from the 1780s, all vase-shaped, double-handled with covers and of impressive size, and all came to Mansion House between 1938 and 1950.

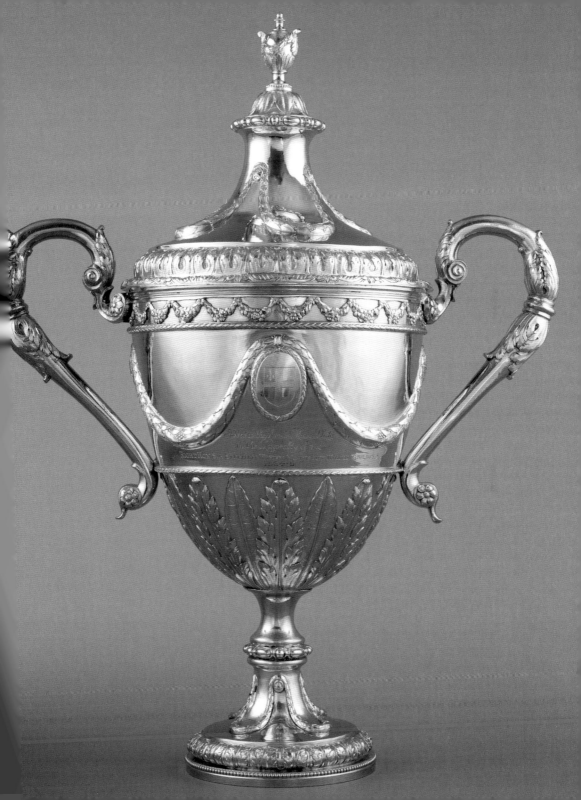

21

Four tureens, lids and stands

John Scofield, London, 1789–90
Silver, 26.7 cm high, 11340 gm gross
Ordered in William Pickett's year (LM 1789–90)

Lord Mayor Pickett was a goldsmith in partnership with Philip Rundell at the sign of
the Golden Salmon on Ludgate Hill until he retired in 1786 to attend to City matters.
Rundell took up with his leading apprentice John Bridge to form the famous firm of
Rundell & Bridge, soon to be joined by Rundell's nephew and become Rundell, Bridge
& Rundell. Pickett, when ordering fine table silver for Mansion House, would certainly
have known the best makers to go to directly, cutting out the retailer. He chose John
Scofield for the task of supplying these tureens and six matching sauce tureens, to which
six more were added in 1815. Scofield was a pre-eminent and talented designer and an
excellent craftsman, though the restrained taste of the period, so beautifully demonstrated
here, prevented him from displaying the virtuosity which might well have given him a
reputation to equal Paul de Lamerie's of an earlier age or Paul Storr's of a later.

The long oval form of the tureens is accentuated by the widely looped handles that join
the body with sprigs of laurel, repeated on the downward curve of the thinning handles
and in a tight band around the bowl. An elegant raised pad at the height of the loops acts
as a thumb rest when being carried. The finely raised fluting on the lids is matched on the
lower body of the bowl, while the ownership by the City is celebrated in the cast and chased
full achievement of the City arms and the winged crests on the lids.

Combining practicality and usefulness with elegant and impressive design, such pieces
were essential at the Lord Mayor's table both for intimate dinners for civic leaders and on
State occasions. These several pieces complemented the plates and serving dishes already at
Mansion House supplied by Paul de Lamerie over 50 years before. The design was evidently
regarded as worth retaining as half a dozen more sauce-tureens were ordered from Richard
Sibley 25 years later.

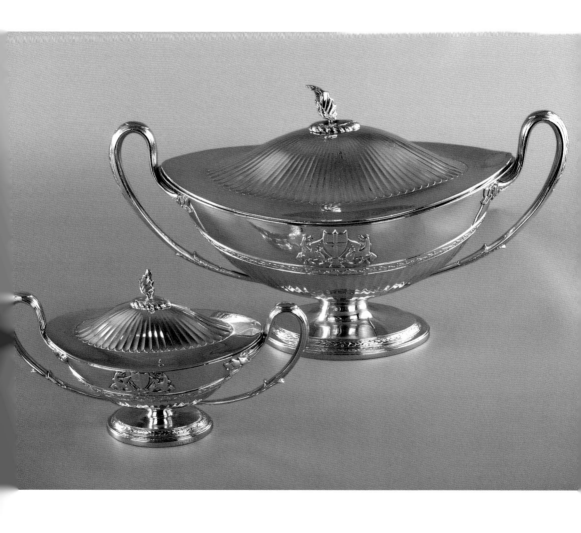

22

Eight ice-pails

Six William Pitts, London, 1799–1800, two Richard Atkins & William Somersall, London, 1833
Silver, 19.7 cm high, 25730 gm gross
Six ordered by Harvey Combe (LM 1799–1800)

The Court of Aldermen ordered a quantity of silver for Mansion House during Harvey
Combe's Mayoral year, including tea and coffee urns, now used as cups (no. 24), the Great
Tray (no. 23) and six wine-bottle coolers, to which were added two more of identical design
in 1833. Inscriptions around the rim give these details in the typical fashion of Mansion
House plate, recording the names and dates of the Lord Mayors involved with the creation,
renovation and restoration of the pieces. Severely Neoclassical, the ice-pails are formed as
tapering buckets with three hoops. Bacchic masks are on either side of the rims as handles,
and a cast and chased border of scrolling vines is around the tops. The pierced liners protect
the bodies and allow the chilled bottles to be removed with ease. The cast and chased
elements that include the City arms on one side and City crest on the other, elongated to
fill the topmost band of the pail, are crisp and delicate. This model is unusual for William
Pitts, who tended towards a more elaborate style for coolers, often of campagna-shape with
more decoration, but the slightly sombre and simplistic form of the design is in keeping
with the setting for which they were intended.

   Harvey Combe, a fabulously wealthy brewer and moderately radical Whig MP for the
City from 1796 until 1817, had been passed over for the Mayoralty several times until he
was at last elected in 1799. The diarist Joseph Farington remarked that "The connexion
with the City has been attended with great expense to him, and he has the honour for it
but not profit". Combe's additions to the silver at Mansion House reflect his determination
to enjoy his year.

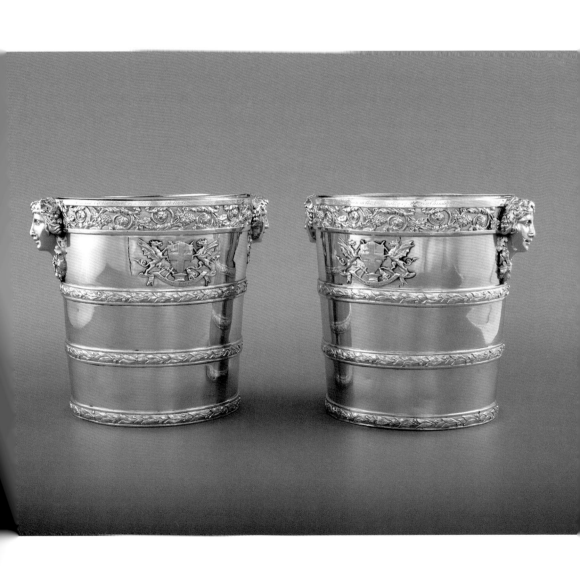

23

The Great Tray

Thomas Hannam & John Crouch, London, 1799–1800
Silver, 110.5 cm long, 64 cm wide, 15629 gm
Ordered by Harvey Combe (LM 1799–1800)

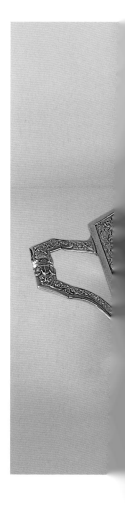

One of the most magnificent pieces of silver at Mansion House, this tray is also one of the most impractical. Fully laden, it would need at least four people to carry it. It reflects both the immense confidence of the City at the end of the eighteenth century and the character of the then Lord Mayor and master brewer Harvey Combe.

Thomas Hannam was apprenticed to William Café, maker of the set of candlesticks at Mansion House (no. 17). He went into partnership with the much younger John Crouch in the 1760s and had a virtual monopoly on the making of trays and salvers from then onwards. Constructing a tray of such dimensions is as much a feat of engineering as it is of smithing, given that the surface will be required to support not only itself but the weight of additional items placed upon it. The base, formed from a single rolled sheet, once riveted to the border then needed to be hammered applying tympanic tension, a highly skilled endeavour. The original hammer marks are still visible on the underside. Handles, wide enough for two hands, are decorated with the same scrolled vines and flower heads as the rim. The centre of the tray is beautifully engraved with the City arms, in pristine condition, reflecting little use.

Though the tray is never used now, the current Mansion House footman can remember it been used for ornamental purposes by a previous Steward, who would serve tea from it.

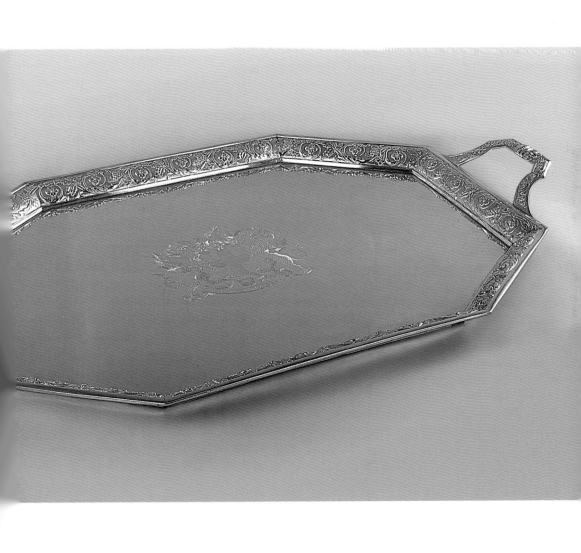

24

The Combe Cups, Covers and Stands

William Pitts, London, 1799–1800
Silver-gilt, 56 cm high, 7233 gm; 47 cm, 6423 gm
Presented by Harvey Combe (LM 1799–1800)

These vases were originally made as a tea urn – the larger – and a coffee urn – the smaller.
At an unknown date the spigots were removed, along with the internal sleeves that held
the iron 'pigs' used to heat the contents. Cast and engraved arms of the City are added
to the double-snake handles, the applied acanthus leaves and the bands of raised and
engraved decoration on the stands, feet and lids. The arms are complemented by the City
crest of a dragon's wing charged with a cross, three-dimensionally and imaginatively made
as a pair of wings to act as knops to the lids.

William Pitts, having moved to new workshops off Lincoln's Inn Fields, had dissolved
his partnership with Joseph Preedy when these cups were made. Versatile and inventive,
he was able to work in a variety of historicizing styles, copying Huguenot work of the
1720s, Paul de Lamerie models and even, in exact replicas, the plastic Rococo designs of
Charles Frederick Kandler. During his year Lord Mayor Harvey Combe also commissioned
Pitts to make six silver ice-pails for the Mansion House (no. 22), and Thomas Hannam
& John Crouch to make the silver Great Tray (no. 23). Combe, MP for the City from 1796,
drew his wealth from the Gyfford Brewery, which eventually became Watney Mann. He
occupied the office of Lord Mayor with great ceremony, as these pieces testify, though his
own portrait commissioned in his Mayoral year was by the distinctly undistinguished
Benjamin Burnell. Friend of the Prince of Wales and a lavish host and gambler, he was also
an enthusiast for pugilism.

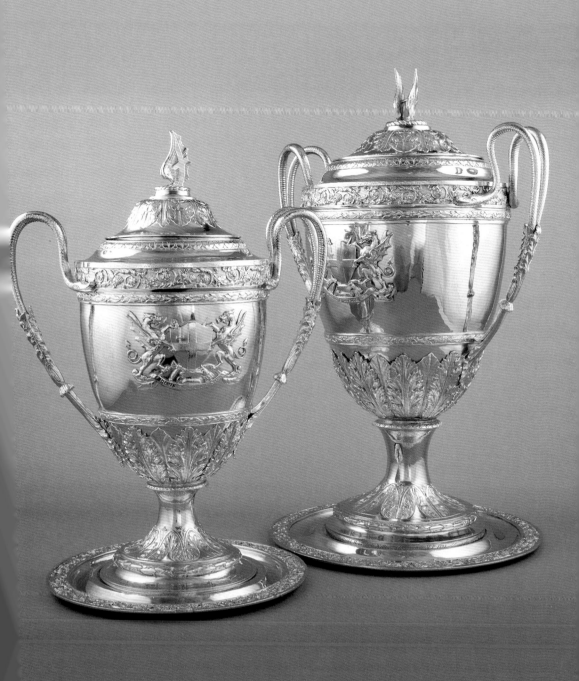

25

Two tureens, lids and stands

Digby Scott and Benjamin Smith for Rundell, Bridge & Rundell, London, 1803–04
Silver, 50.8 cm high, 15620 gm gross
Ordered in Sir John Eamer's year (LM 1801–02)

Banquets at Mansion House in the late eighteenth century had table decorations made of sugar sculptures, fruit and flowers. Only gradually did the City acquire silver of significant quality to act both usefully and decoratively. The four tureens acquired in the 1780s (no. 21), though large and impressive, were still purely functional rather than decorative, made without stands and with large, looped handles for ease when serving. The silver ordered in Sir John Eamer's year marks a turning point for the Mansion House plate collection, when hugely impressive pieces were ordered that transcended simple service wares and glorified the wealth and success of the City: these tureens and their associated silver-gilt sauceboats (no. 26) fulfil that function.

The overall design, attributable to the young French designer Jean-Jacques Boileau, recalls the fashionable Parisian work of Henri Auguste, particularly the heavy beading round the foot and the fully three-dimensional winged figures as handles, here holding the City Sword and Mace, though the mace is not an accurate representation but merely a rod bearing an arched crown. The lids are surmounted by seated figures emblematic of the City of London, the shield of the City resting by their sides. The addition of the City arms, backed by elaborate mantelling, cast and chased to the highest quality, confirm that this was a direct commission of the very highest order. However, there is still an echo of the *goût Grec*, the heavy Neoclassicism that developed in France in the 1760s and early 1770s but which quickly gave way to a more refined version of the style. The solid beading and the substantial profile of the stand and the almost free-flying handles recall French designs by Jean-Guillaume Moitte and Pierre Gouthière of the 1780s.

A small number of similarly magnificent tureens all associated with Rundell, Bridge & Rundell exist, including a very similar set of four made for them by Paul Storr in the Gilbert Collection, commissioned by the Duke of Cumberland but in an Egyptian manner. They all appear to derive from a tureen made by Auguste in the late 1790s and supplied to the British Crown. They are highly impractical for their intended purpose of holding soups or stews, indeed it is hard to imagine how they could be used as vessels at all. In keeping with the luxury and grandeur of the dawning Regency, however, they certainly make an imposing decorative statement.

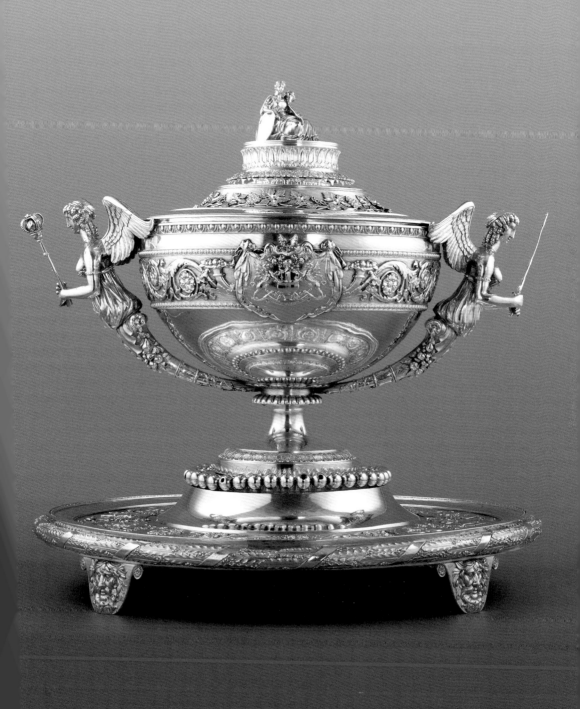

26

Six sauce tureens and covers

Digby Scott and Benjamin Smith for Rundell, Bridge & Rundell, London, 1803–04
Silver-gilt, the vases 51 cm high, 7006 gm
Ordered in Sir John Eamer's year (LM 1801–02)

Hemispherical bowls, standing on circular feet with waterleaf borders, have detached handles rising on either side that terminate in female busts, their shoulders wreathed with leaves and berries. A band of cast and chased decoration runs round the body of the bowl, with paired cornucopiae against a matted ground and the arms of the City backed by the crossed Mace and Sword on either side. The flat lids are decorated with handles in the form of tightly coiled snakes. These sauce tureens were made en suite with the pair of large and more elaborate silver soup tureens (no. 25) also by Scott and Smith for Rundell, Bridge & Rundell, all to designs probably done by the talented French designer Jean-Jacques Boileau.

Boileau came to London from Paris in c. 1787, initially as a decorative painter to work on the Prince of Wales's Carlton House, then being rebuilt and decorated by Henry Holland. Under Holland's patronage he is known to have designed and painted interiors for a number of prestigious clients, including the 6th Duke of Bedford at Woburn, William Beckford at Fonthill and, with Augustus Pugin, George IV at Windsor. A large group of designs for silver in the Victoria and Albert Museum link him conclusively to pieces made for Rundell, Bridge & Rundell very similar to these tureens, with simple, geometric outlines, heavily Greek and Egyptian decorative motifs, crisply cast and chased, ultimately derived from the 1770s designs of the French silversmith Henri Auguste. Auguste himself drew on the many newly excavated ceramic and metal objects from Herculaneum that were published extensively in the 1770s, often under the patronage of the King of Naples, brother-in-law to Queen Marie-Antoinette. The Paris-Naples axis was extended by amateurs and collectors from England, Grand Tourists, or diplomats like Sir William Hamilton. Boileau, studying these publications and Auguste's work in France, may well have been responsible for the initial design of an immensely popular candlestick, known in a number of variations, four of which are at Mansion House and compliment these tureens (see no. 27).

Inscriptions on the sauce tureens and the stands of the soup tureens record that these pieces were made in the mayoralty of Sir John Eamer, no doubt at the order of the Common Council and clearly not at Sir John's expense. They were the first pieces of grand ceremonial plate to be provided for the Mansion House since the first deliveries of plates and dishes by Paul de Lamerie, and they mark a new confidence and prosperity in the City. Sir John Eamer, a wealthy grocer and Master of the Salters' Company, was, like many of his class and rank in an age of great military and naval exploits, a colonel of a regiment of the East London Militia. After his Mayoral year he moved to Brighton and died in 1823, unmourned.

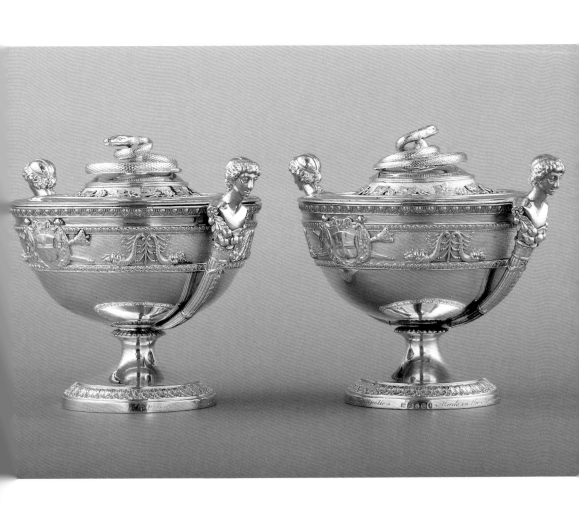

27

Two three-light candelabra and two four-light candelabra

Benjamin & James Smith and Benjamin Smith, London, 1809–10, 1810–11 (two) and 1827–28
Silver-gilt, 68.5 cm high, 8025 gm each
First ordered during the year of Thomas Smith (LM 1809–10)

Originally supplied between 1809 and 1810, one four-light and two three-light candelabra
were joined by a second four-light example some seventeen years later. The orders for
their purchase fell during a number of mayoralties from 1809 onwards. They are a model
designed for Rundell, Bridge & Rundell, who were by this date silversmiths to the Prince
Regent and pre-eminent in the production of the most luxurious and opulent silver for
the Court and the City. This model was produced in a number of variants from about 1804
to 1815. Several elements of the design, particularly the branches, can be attributed to the
Frenchman Jean-Jacques Boileau (see no. 26).

Standing on simple, highly polished triangular plinths, the muscular lion's jamb legs
spring from foliated bosses, which support the fluted tapering shaft of the sticks. The
model for these legs was drawn directly from a bronze Roman candelabrum first published
in 1792. The shafts, engraved on the plain central section with the City arms, stand on three
pairs of human feet. The papyrus capitals support three Greek-style heads, from which
rise the inverted bell-shaped supports for the detachable arms. The mixture of classical
and ancient Egyptian motifs – immensely popular in Europe after the Anglo-French war
in Egypt at the beginning of the century – extends to the palmette, rosette and berried
elements of the arms, which sweep up to the purely Neoclassical gadrooning of the exterior
of the drip-pans and the candle-holders themselves.

Benjamin Smith II, originally from Birmingham, where he worked with Matthew
Boulton, moved to London by 1802 and briefly went into partnership with his brother
James between 1809 and 1812. He had been manager of Rundell & Bridge's silver workshops
in Greenwich since 1802, before Paul Storr took over and moved them to Soho in 1807.
Famously irascible, he had returned to working alone when commissioned to make the
single four-light example in 1827.

So popular was this model that it was made by a large number of different
manufacturers, all working in some way under the control of Rundell, Bridge & Rundell.
There are 24 four-light candelabra without the triangular stands made in 1804–08 and
1812–13 in the Royal Collection, for example. The firm had close contacts with the City
hierarchy (see no. 21).

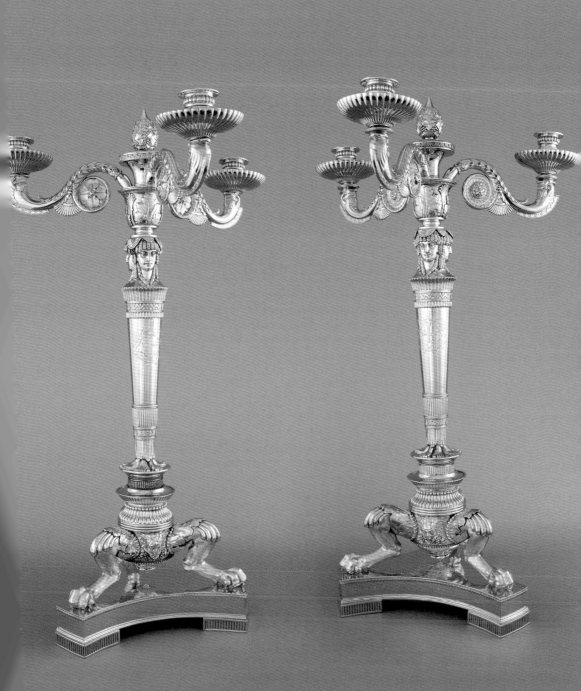

28

The Studd Cup and Cover

Philip Rundell for Rundell, Bridge & Rundell, London, 1821–22
Silver-gilt, 46 cm high, 5925 gm
Made for King George IV; acquired in 1924 by Sir Kynaston Studd (LM 1928–29)

The plinth of this cup and cover, rectangular in form, stands on four short fluted feet, the panels at the front and back decorated with the royal arms of England, as borne by the house of Hanover from 1816 to 1837. On it stands a campagna-shaped double-handled vase, the roll-moulded foot, decorated with cast and chased rosettes, rising on a short stem to a gadrooned and beaded ring that supports the unusually short body of the vase. Ultimately derived from the kylix form of Greek krater, this vase emphasizes the Greek rather than Roman elements of the design, particularly in the smooth, tapering diminution of the scrolling handles and the waterleaf and flower-head design of the lower body. A cast and applied relief on one side of a seated woman and child – possibly a reference to the baptism the cup celebrates – is attributable to John Flaxman, who worked both for Rundells and for the Wedgwood manufactory. The cast and chased British Imperial crown resting on a cushion that forms the knop to the lid indicates a royal commission, as the inscription on the reverse, in eight different fonts, recalls. Philip Rundell, an eccentric and unpleasant character, retired from business soon after this cup was made with a reputed fortune of over £1 million, made largely at the expense of the Prince Regent, George IV, his greatest and most extravagant client.

This cup was presented by George IV in 1821 to the Russian ambassador Count Lieven and his wife to celebrate the baptism of their son George Frederick Alexander, for whom the King stood sponsor. It is reputed that George IV was in fact the boy's father, which might explain the lavish nature of the gift. An inscription on the two sides of the plinth further record that the cup, having been stolen from the ambassador's descendants during the Russian revolution of 1917, was clandestinely offered to Sir Kynaston Studd, Bt (LM 1928–29) while he was on honeymoon with his second wife, Princess Alexandra Lieven, in Paris in 1924. Sir Kynaston acquired the cup and presented it to the Mansion House plate collection in 1929 to commemorate his Mayoral year. A noted evangelical with no business ties to the City, he had been encouraged to seek office by his close friend Quintin Hogg and other colleagues at the Regent's Street Polytechnic, of which he was President and which received much financial support from City charities. He lavishly entertained distinguished cricketers at the Mansion House during his year.

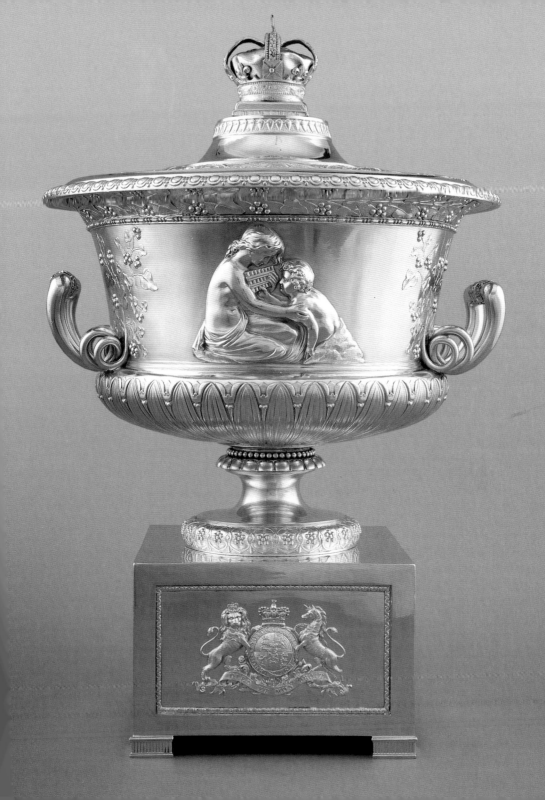

29

The Salomons Salver

Jonathan Hayne, London, 1824
Silver, 62 cm diameter, 6210 gm
Purchased by the Court of Aldermen, 2003

This very large and very heavy salver has a richly cast and chased rim, with pairs of eagles facing each other alternating with pairs of winged *amorini* playing a variety of musical instruments, all set in foliate scrolls of flowers, predominantly roses. The iconography might refer to the amorous associations of the salver, celebrating the marriage of David Salomons to Jeanette Cohen on 23 April 1823. Salomons, who was twenty-six at the time, went on to become one of the most prominent bankers and stockbrokers of the Victorian age. Miss Cohen was the niece of both N.M. Rothschild and Sir Moses Montefiore, leading figures of the London Jewish community.

Soon after his marriage Salomons began a highly idiosyncratic war of attrition on City and national institutions that barred Jews from holding office. He was eventually admitted to a livery company, the Coopers, and then held the office of Sheriff in 1835, becoming a magistrate in 1838 and an Alderman in 1845. In 1851 he stood successfully for Parliament at a by-election in Greenwich. When he took the oath in the Commons he omitted references to Christianity, and on taking his seat he immediately voted in the three divisions that followed before he was persuaded to withdraw. He was more successful in the City, where he was elected the first Jewish Lord Mayor in 1855-56. He was created a Baronet in 1869. His wife predeceased him and they had no children. The salver is engraved in the centre with the arms of Salomons on the left impaled by Cohen on the right.

Jonathan Hayne was apprenticed to and then in partnership with Thomas Wallis II, a scion of an old established silversmithing family. With premises in Clerkenwell, he was working alone by the 1820s – apparently very successfully, as he had a number of registered apprentices and went on to become Prime Warden of the Goldsmiths' Company in 1848. The rim of this salver shows the nineteenth century's increasing interest in historicizing styles, particularly in Renaissance motifs. A large flat area has been left unadorned for the addition of heraldry as required. The salver was purchased by the General Purposes Committee of the Court of Aldermen in 2003 for inclusion in the Mansion House plate collection in recognition of the City's first Jewish Lord Mayor.

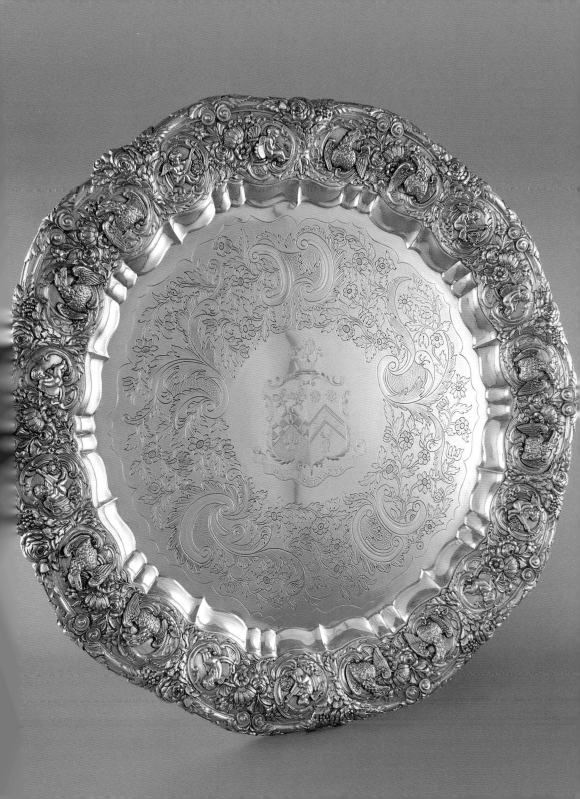

30

The Bowater Wine Cooler

Robert Garrard, London, 1830–31
Silver-gilt, 30.5 cm high, 5536 gm
Bears the initial 'C' below a marquis's coronet within a motto garter,
for the 2nd Duke of Buckingham while Marquis of Chandos
Presented by Messrs Guest, Keen and Nettlefold to Sir Ian Bowater (LM 1969–70)
and presented by him to the City

This magnificent wine cooler formed part of a service of plate presented in 1832 to the licentious and thoroughly dissolute Marquis of Chandos, later 2nd Duke of Buckingham, when he successfully led the Parliamentary campaign for the enfranchisement of £50 tenants-at-will, giving the vote to thousands of tenant farmers. Grateful tenants on his father's estates in Buckinghamshire presented the young Marquis with a service of plate weighing some 2000 oz, of which this cooler, along with five others of the same design, formed a part. This example is numbered 2 on the body and on the elaborately pierced liner, and is also marked up for the correct position to insert the sleeve into the body. Later, when the bankrupted Duke sold the contents of his great house at Stowe at auction in 1848, the tenantry bought the service back for him.

Made by the leading silversmith of the day Robert Garrard, successor in silver fashion to Rundell, Bridge & Rundell, the design played on an acquatic theme, using four dolphins with raised tails to support the spiral fluted body, which rises from rippling waves of the calix to the rim of shells and waterweeds.

The luxury and extravagance of this cooler would have appealed immensely to Lord Chandos. At the 1848 sale that marked his nadir, The Times thundered: "A man of the highest rank, and of a property not unequal to his title, has flung all away by extravagance and folly, and reduced his honours to the tinsel of a pauper and the bauble of a fool". The coolers, retained by the family, were eventually sold in 1964. Through the friendship of Sir Trevor Holdsworth, who had begun his career in the Bowater group of companies and became a senior director of Guest, Keen & Nettlefold, Sir Ian Bowater briefly became a director of GKN Birfield, a relationship which prompted the gift of this cooler to Sir Ian and his onward gift to the Mansion House plate collection.

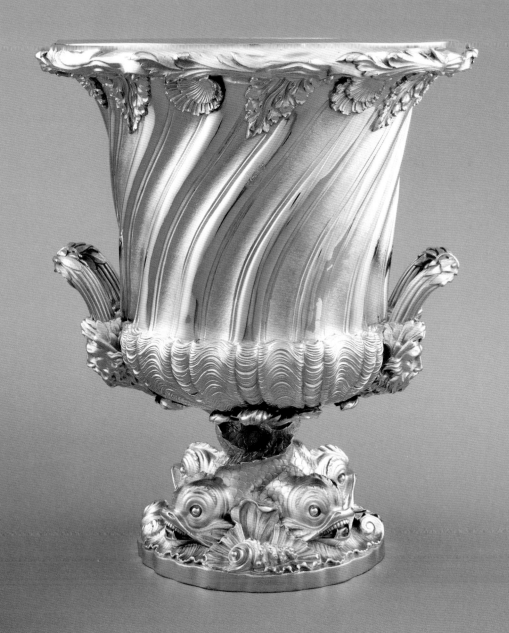

31

Queen Victoria's knife and fork

KNIFE William Theobalds & Robert Atkinson, London, 1838–39
FORK William Trayes, London, 1837–38
Silver-gilt and porcelain, the knife 18.4 cm long, the fork 15.9 cm long
Presented by Queen Mary, 1936

Queen Mary was an inveterate habituée of antique shops. *The Times* of 5 February 1937 recorded that the Queen had sent the Lord Mayor of London, Sir George Broadbridge (LM 1937–38), a knife and fork that she had recently found, wondering if they were part of a set already at Mansion House that had been made for Queen Victoria. The Lord Mayor showed them to James Lungley Douthwaite, curator at the Guildhall, who declared the porcelain Coalport and commented on the unusual iconography of the City arms and royal crown, but said they were not from a set made for the Mansion House. He also pointed out that a spoon, now lost, probably completed the set. *The Times* did not report, however, that the Queen subsequently graciously presented them to Mansion House.

The careful use of the word 'probably' in the inscription inside the case reflects the fact that the dates of the marks do not tally with the magnificent State Banquet given at the Guildhall on 9 November 1837 to Queen Victoria nor with the date of the Coronation on 28 June the following year, though Queen Victoria did attend a supper at Mansion House in 1840. Therefore, "probably made to commemorate a Royal visit to the City" is as much detail as one may ever get.

The porcelain handle, with a green ground and diaper pattern in gold with reserves of flowers, is based on an eighteeth-century Sèvres model, though the bulbous form is nineteenth-century English and, as Douthwaite noted, it probably originated from the Minton or Coalport porcelain manufactories. Theobalds & Atkinson and Trayes were well-known flatware makers in the early nineteenth century, though why the young Queen Victoria would have used a fork with the City arms cast and chased is unclear. Queen Mary may well have presented these pieces to the Mansion House plate collection in thanks for the Lord Mayor Sir Percy Vincent's highly successful appeal to raise a national memorial to her late husband, King George V, who had died in January 1936.

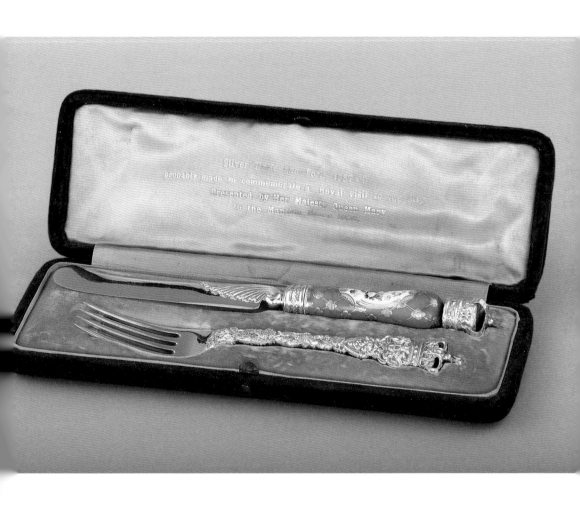

Silver ???? ... ...
probably made to commemorate a Royal visit to the City
Presented by Her Majesty Queen Mary
to the Mansion House ????

32

The Wilson Epergne

Edward Barnard & Sons, London, 1839–40
Silver-gilt, 86.3 cm high, 15801 gm
Presented to Colonel Samuel Wilson (LM 1839–40) by his fellow citizens and friends
and presented by his trustees in 1881

Lord Mayor elect Wilson (the incumbent, Lord Mayor Cowan, was ill) carried the Crystal
Sceptre (no. 1) at the coronation of Queen Victoria in 1838. Elected at a comparatively early
age – he was just forty-two – Wilson lived until he was ninety. He clearly made a significant
mark on City affairs, as a month after leaving office a public meeting held at the London
Coffee House formed a committee to raise funds for a public testimonial in his honour.
This centrepiece, full of the pride of a great trading City at the dawn of the Victoria era, was
the result.

The triangular scrolled base with large cartouches inscribed and engraved with the City
arms and those of Wilson are flanked by the City dragons in a fairly conventional design.
The plinth that they form, however, supports three cast figures – a seated personification
of London, a standing figure of Commerce holding a steelyard balance, and the figure of
Plenty with cornucopiae of specie and fruit – all in the shade of three large palm trees. Out
of the crowns of these trees sprout eight scrolled candle arms and a grape-wreathed bowl
in the centre.

A colonel in the Royal London Militia, Wilson was an Alderman for the Wards of Castle
Barnard and Bridge Without and a member of the Weavers' Company – none of which
explains the palm trees, unless they are a reference to the world-wide trade of the City of
London. Lord Mayor Wilson was popular not only with the City but also with his own
extensive and prosperous family, signified by a banquet he and his wife hosted during
his year: "The Wilson banquet took place in April 1839. For the occasion the Egyptian Hall
was decorated with unusual splendour: – and as it was not so crowded as on ordinary State
Banquets. The scene was very fine. Invitations had been sent out to nearly two hundred
connections of the Wilson Family being above the age of nine years; only two exceptions on
the point of age being permitted, one the grandson of Bishop Wilson of Calcutta, and the
other a favorite nephew, six years old, who acted as page to the Lord Mayor." The trustees
of Colonel Wilson deposited the centrepiece at Mansion House after his death in 1881.

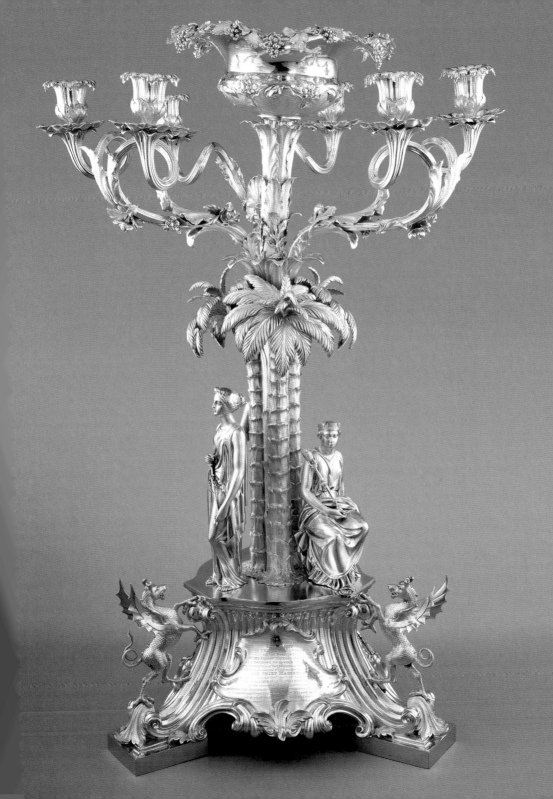

33

The Farncombe Snuff Box

Charles Rawlings & William Summers, London, 1849
Silver-gilt, 15.8 cm long, 10.8 cm wide, 6 cm high, 1306 gm
Presented by Thomas Farncombe (LM 1849–50)

This magnificent box of exceptional quality has slightly canted sides and a lid framed with
cast and chased fruit, flowers and leaves, finely engraved with strapwork showing a scene
of a medieval king on a busy trading wharf – a reference to the then Lord Mayor's principal
occupation. The City arms are also cast and chased to a very high quality. An inscription
on the base records that the box was ordered during the Mayoralty of Thomas Farncombe
in 1849, and this is repeated on the lids of the two compartments, revealed when the lid
is opened. A wealthy wharfinger and ship-owner, Farncomb presided at a banquet at
Mansion House at which Prince Albert announced the Great Exhibition to be held in Hyde
Park in 1851. He was one of the very few bachelor Lord Mayors.

   The partnership of Rawlings & Summers, based in Brook Street, off High Holborn,
produced high quality smallwork, notably flatware, wine tickets and snuff boxes, this
being a fine example of their work.

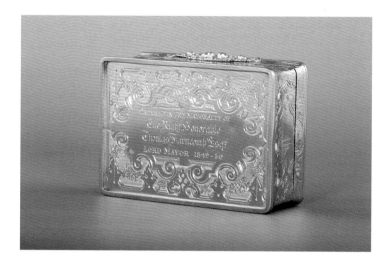

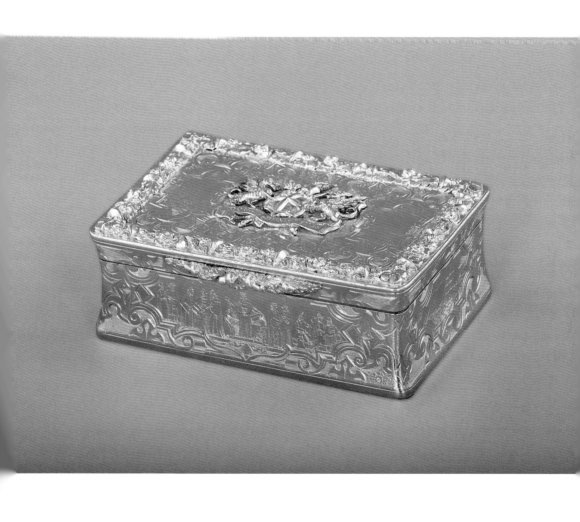

34

The Bower Cup and Cover

Robert Hennell IV, London, 1869–70
Silver-gilt, 91.5 cm high, 6345 gm
Presented by Sir Alfred Bower, Bt (LM 1924–25)

This extraordinary cup and cover, combining Gothic and Renaissance forms and motifs with Neoclassical three-dimensional figures, expresses the assurance of High Victorian eclecticism as well as the early twentieth-century social confidence that led Sir Alfred Bower to present it to Mansion House after his year in office. The silver foot, body and lid are raised and lavishly decorated with cast and chased silver-gilt elements, culminating in the silver figure of winged Fame blowing a trumpet. It is based more on the elaborate drinking cups found in Europe in the sixteenth and seventeenth centuries than the sober designs of Robert Adam and the Enlightenment usually seen in the City. The semi-naked figures of children recline within silver-gilt tendrils of exuberant handles that recal jewellery designs by Dürer or Holbein. The handles emphasize the breadth of the body of the cup in comparison to the narrowness of the stem below. At nearly a metre high it can hardly go unnoticed. Robert Hennell, the fourth Robert in a distinguished family of English silversmiths dating back to the early eighteenth century, inherited the manufacturing firm at his father's death in 1869. He clearly wished to make an impression early in his proprietorship. The cup also bears a mark of a vertical 'H' overlaid by a horizontal 'H' that may reflect the close relationship of Robert Hennell with the retailers Hancock & Co., possibly unique in English silver and added post assay.

It was probably the Continental and slightly libidinous feel that attracted Sir Alfred to this cup when looking for a suitable offering to the Mansion House plate collection after his year in 1925. In the aftermath of the Great War the Lord Mayor made a visit to Paris and Verdun, receiving both the Légion d'Honneur and the Freedom of the City of Verdun, events recorded by inscription on this cup. Sir Alfred founded the wine merchants Bower & Co. in 1879, and owned several of the earliest wine bars, the first in Mark Lane off Fenchurch Street and later on Fleet Street. Told that if he was elected Lord Mayor he must cease trading under his own name, he changed 'Bower's' to 'El Vino' in 1923; El Vino remains a popular City venue to this day.

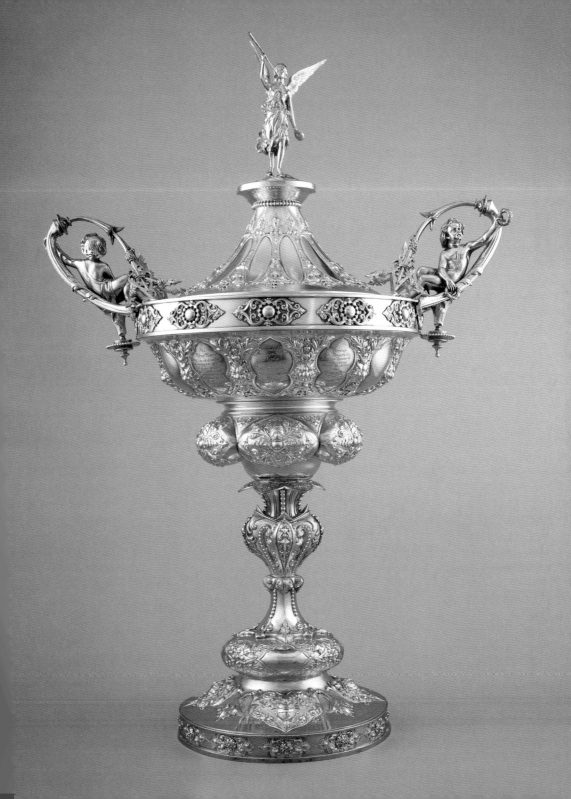

35

The Epping Forest Testimonial

Edward Barnard & Sons, London, 1879–80
Silver and glass, 59 cm high, 4389 gm
Bequeathed by John Bedford in 1900

The rapid expansion of London suburbs in the second half of the nineteenth century put pressure for enclosure on the ancient royal forest of Waltham, now called Epping Forest, on the borders of London and Essex. Nibblings had reduced the forest in size from over 12,000 acres at the beginning of the eighteenth century to 6,000 acres in 1850 and a mere 3,500 acres by 1870. Things came to a head in 1865 when the Revd William Maitland, lord of the manor of Loughton, enclosed 1,100 acres, and the commoners, who had grazing and lopping rights, vigorously protested. For over ten years legal battles and negotiations continued. The City, which held ancient sporting and recreational rights, bought Aldersbrook Farm (now a cemetery) within the forest boundaries, gaining commoner status and thereby joining the case against the feudal landlords, which was decisively won in the Court of Chancery in 1872. This prevented further enclosure and eventually returned land enclosed since 1851, creating the area of mixed farm, heath and woodland of some 6,100 acres today. Furthermore, the City bought out the lords of the manors, and finally, in 1878, the Epping Forest Act brought the entire forest into the care of the City, where it has remained ever since. In 2012 the area of Epping Forest was increased for the first time since the Act in 1878, through the acquisition by the City of 30 acres of land, which were planted with trees to make Gifford Wood, named for Sir Roger Gifford (LM 2012–13).

In 1871 City Deputy John Bedford proposed a motion in Common Council that "a committee be appointed to seek to ascertain on what terms and conditions the Corporation can secure to the people, for purposes of public health and recreation, those parts of Epping Forest which have not been enclosed". Described as a "Gentleman Merchant, residing in Mecklenburgh Square", Bedford secured the recovery of 3,000 acres of illegally enclosed land in 1874, and the motion was followed eventually by the 1878 Act. In gratitude for his work in the cause of the forest, a public subscription raised funds for this magnificent epergne to be made by the leading City silversmiths, Barnards, who supplied so much silver to Mansion House during the nineteenth century. The scrolled feet decorated with ferns rise to a triangular base, on which stand and sit models of three red deer, which were then native to the forest. From their midst rise oak branches terminating in three candle-holders and supporting a nest of oak leaves and twigs containing a cut-glass bowl. Plaques on three sides record the circumstances, the initials and the arms of John Bedford, who bequeathed it at his death in 1900, aged eighty-seven, to the Mansion House plate collection.

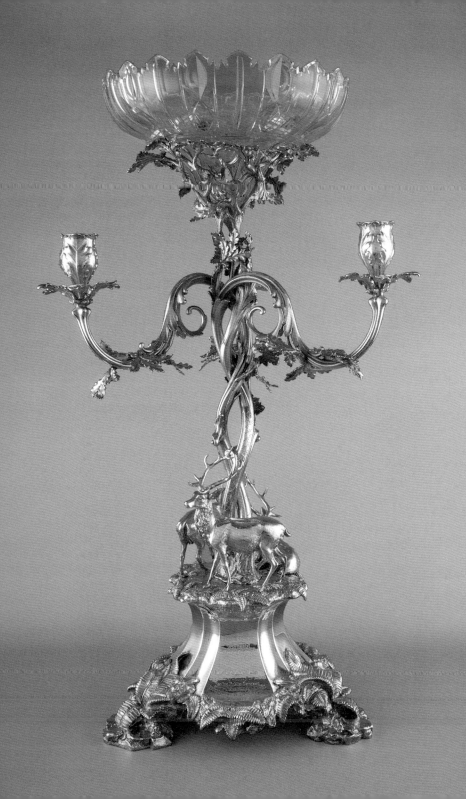

36

The Great Centrepiece and Stand and six-piece garniture

Robert Garrard II, London, 1880–81

CENTREPIECE ON STAND Silver, 123 cm long, 19004 gm gross
TWO SMALLER COMPANIONS Silver, each 92.25 cm long, 22550 gm gross
FOUR DESERT STANDS Silver, each 36.2 cm long, 8762 gm gross

Victorian confidence on land and sea, the growing Empire and the trade and wealth
it brought to the City are here made in silver. In three cast and chased sections, each
centrepiece has two figures representative of the dominant position of the City in world
trade. The central plateau has figures of Commerce and of Navigation, who rests beside a
small column containing a real compass, while figures emblematic of Africa, Asia, America
and Europe take up the world trade theme. Heavily Neoclassical in style, with gadrooning,
scrolling, swags and egg-and-dart decoration, the pieces reflect the grandeur and solidity
of current architectural styles in the City and beyond. Their practical use is evident in the
long but very low design, intended for the narrow tables used in the Egyptian Hall, where
tall decorations would obscure and obstruct conversation. Low arrangements of fruit and
flowers can be made in the pierced integral bowls of each section. The date of 1881 is also
significant in the history of Garrards, marking the death of Robert Garrard II and the
beginning of a steady decline in their silver trade in favour of manufacturing and retailing
jewellery.

The Great Centrepiece was ordered during the Mayoralty of Sir William MacArthur
(LM 1880–81), whose considerable success as a trader is admirably represented in the
iconography and sheer weight of silver in the centrepiece. Trade at the time was the
backbone of City prosperity, and in 1881 the Royal Albert Dock was opened, nearly
doubling the size of wharfage for London commerce. At the opening of the Albert Dock
The Times noted that "In no single spot of London, not even at the Bank, could so vivid an
impression of the vast wealth of England be obtained as at the Docks". MacArthur had
established a woollens export business in his native Londonderry in the 1830s, and had
greatly prospered through his family contacts in Australia, allowing him to open a London
office in 1858. Devoutly Methodist, MacArthur used his considerable influence in the
City to promote both international trade and missionary work in the colonies. He avidly
supported the abolition of slavery and the suppression of the opium trade – ideas that were
typical of Non-Conformist Liberals of the day.

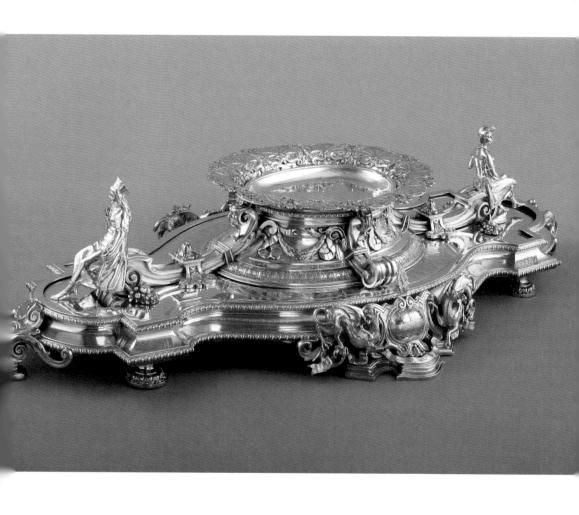

37
The Cripplegate Cup and Cover

Edward Barnard & Sons, London, 1883–84
Silver-gilt, 47 cm high, 3250 gm
Presented by Sir Henry Knight (LM 1882–83) in 1883

This is the earliest of several cups and covers at Mansion House named for the wards of the gifting Aldermen who became Lord Mayor. Sir Henry Knight, who had represented Cripplegate Ward since 1867, complemented the City's recent acquisition of Epping Forest by adding two more open spaces to the City's property, Burnham Beeches in Buckinghamshire and Coulsden Commons in south London. In November 1882 Sir Henry was the last Lord Mayor to be sworn in at Westminster. He attended the opening of the new Royal Courts of Justice in the Strand in May 1883, where the annual ceremony has since taken place.

Cripplegate, in the centre of the northern walls of the City, now exists only in name, as the entire area was heavily bombed during the Second World War and redeveloped in the 1950s and 1960s as the Barbican. An ancient entrance into the City at the start of the Great North Road, now called the A1, with a brick and ashlar Tudor towered gate, the ward's parish church was dedicated to St Giles, patron saint of cripples. It still stands in splendid isolation within the Barbican complex, one of the few medieval City churches to survive both the Great Fire and the Blitz, though much altered and restored. The reference to cripples is reflected in the two seated figures of limbless mendicants on the foot of the cup, with crutches and caps outstretched. They sit on either side of finely cast medallions showing the Tudor gateway, while two further detachable medallions on the body of the cup show St Giles itself and the old City of London School in Milk Street. Sir Henry, a former pupil of the school and its Captain during his Mayoralty, officiated at the opening of its new building on the Embankment in 1882. The medallions were probably struck by a medallist and inserted by the silversmith into the body of the cup, which has been bent round a form and soldered together, rather than being raised. The arms of the City and those of Sir Henry, both finely cast and chased, flank the plaques on either side of the cup. The curious mixture of styles, Gothic and Neoclassical, actually work well together to reflect the medieval history of the ward, the current improvements of the modern world and Sir Henry's role in the life of London. Handsome City dragons, more elongated than usual, form the handles and gaze admiringly towards the seated figure of London that surmounts the lid.

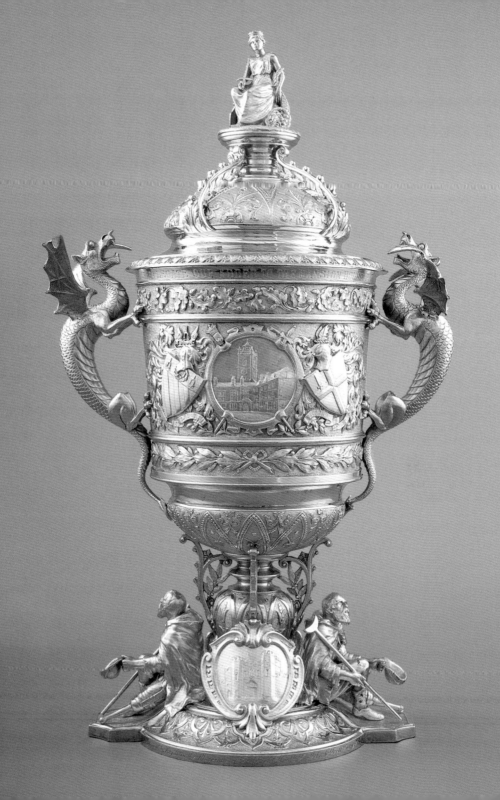

38

The Cornhill Cup and Cover

Edward Barnard & Sons, London, 1884–85
Silver-gilt, 44.5 cm high, 3250 gm
Presented by Sir Robert Fowler, Bt, MP (LM 1883–84 and part of 1885
at the death of George Nottage in office) in 1884

The tradition started by Sir Henry Knight, Sir Robert Fowler's immediate predecessor at
Lord Mayor (see no. 37), of presenting a cup and cover reflecting his ward continued with
this, the Cornhill Cup, the following year. A member of the Spectacle Makers' Company,
Sir Robert was elected Alderman for Cornhill in 1878, where his privately owned family
bank had premises. Born and raised a Quaker, he espoused the Conservative cause and
became an Anglican in later life. Despite a well-meaning social conscience, bred in his
roots, he nevertheless enjoyed fox-hunting on his Wiltshire estate, and as an MP actively
worked against reform of the City. Indeed, a Commons enquiry was found guilty of
'malversation', misusing Corporation funds to fight off reforms during his year in office,
but he avoided prosecution. His long-suffering wife never reached Mansion House; she
died of exhaustion after the birth of eleven children – ten girls and finally a boy. His son-
in-law and biographer commented that "his talents were all of the solid kind: of what is
called brilliance of intellect he possessed almost nothing at all".

Sir Henry was a proud man and chose not to hide his light under a bushel when
commissioning this cup and cover from the famous house of Barnard, goldsmiths to the
City in the late nineteenth century. His coat-of-arms lies prominently at the foot, backed
by the City Mace and Sword, and complemented by his crest in three dimensions on the
lid. The six scenes on the body of the cup represent ancient and modern architectural
highlights of his ward: the modern include the present Royal Exchange, the Drapers'
Company church of St Michael's Cornhill, and Wren's St Peter's-upon-Cornhill, while the
ancient ones are the old Royal Exchange built by Sir Thomas Gresham; the Tun, a medieval
lock-up for street-walkers, scolds and lewd women; and the Standard, a water-conduit used
as a starting point to measure distances from the City.

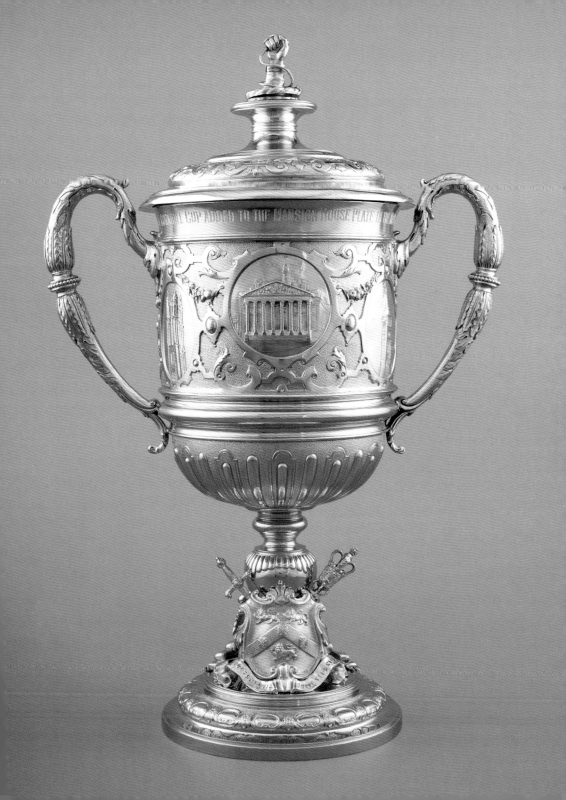

39

The Cordwainer Cup and Cover

Edward Barnard & Sons, London, 1885–86
Silver-gilt, 45.7 cm high, 2848 gm
Presented by Mrs Swan Nottage, widow of George Swan Nottage
(LM 1884–85; died in office)

George Swan Nottage was elected Lord Mayor in November 1884 and died, aged only sixty-two, in April the following year. He had caught a cold while in Brighton just before Easter, returning to the Mansion House for the Bluecoat presentation and the Easter banquet, which was cancelled when the cold turned to pneumonia. It is an ancient right and privilege of Lord Mayors who die in office to be honoured with a civic funeral in St Paul's Cathedral. It is entirely appropriate, therefore, that the cup and cover presented by his widow to commemorate his brief Mayoralty should have been made in the form of the dome of St Paul's. The supporting dragons of the City arms form the handles while two cast and chased reliefs show views of St Mary Aldermary in Cordwainer Ward, and St Mary-le-Bow next to Swan Nottage's office at 54 Cheapside. Seated at the foot of the cup beside two shields – one with the arms of the City, the other with Swan Nottage's arms – are two shoe-makers, reflecting the traditional activity of the ward that the cup represents and copying the mendicants on the foot of Sir Henry Knight's Cripplegate Cup of 1882–83 (no. 37).

Though not a member of the Cordwainers' Company, George Swan Nottage represented the ward as Alderman from 1875 until his death. In 1854 he had founded the London Stereoscopic & Photographic Company, initially selling stereoscopic photographs and the viewers invented by his business associate Sir David Brewster, then branching out into all forms of photography with agents and photographers worldwide. The company held the Royal Warrant as Photographers to Queen Victoria. He was a liveryman of the Loriners', Spectacle Makers' and Carpenters' Companies and was Master of the Carpenters from 1884 to 1885. The first Lord Mayor to die in office since William Beckford in 1770, he was buried with much pomp and a good deal of grief at Kensal Green, and honoured with a commemorative brass in the crypt of St Paul's. Sir Robert Fowler completed the year as Lord Mayor (see no. 38).

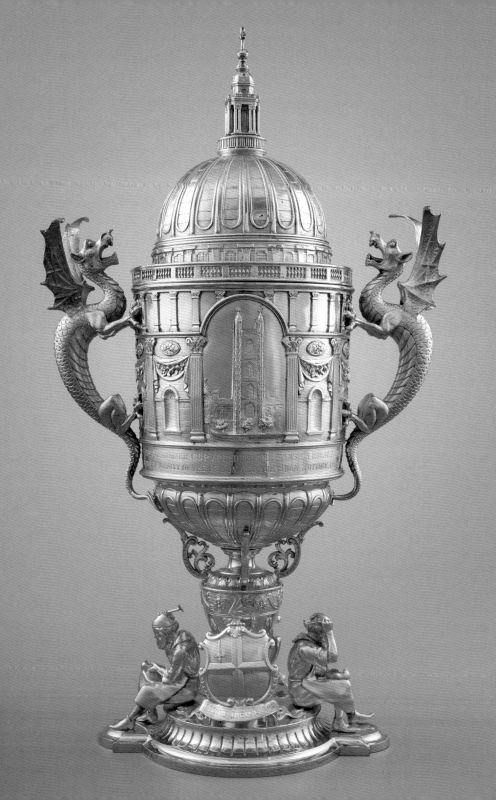

40

The Jubilee Cup and Cover

Edward Barnard & Sons, London, 1886–87, and Toye, Keen & Spencer, 1978
Silver-gilt, 50 cm high, 2665 gm
Presented by Sir Reginald Hanson, Bt (LM 1885–86) to commemorate
Queen Victoria's Golden Jubilee

> *Romans! Let this be your care, this your art;*
> *To rule over the Nations and impose the ways of peace,*
> *To spare the underdog, and pull down the proud.*

These words from the *Aeneid*, quoted by Rudyard Kipling in his *Regulus* of 1917, are reflected in this symbol of an Empire at its peak, even to Kipling's subtitle – *A Diversity of Creatures*. Crowned by an image of Queen Victoria herself, this cup was made to commemorate her Golden Jubilee, celebrated on 20 June 1887. The figure of the Queen on the lid is modelled on the work of Charles Bell Birch, first produced at life-size for Aberdeen at the Jubilee and subsequently recast in 1893 for Blackfriars Bridge. The barrel-shaped body of the cup is set with four oval panels in relief representing India, Canada, Africa and Australia, a theme repeated on the foot, which teems with wildlife: a lion, tiger, beaver and kangaroo are overlooked by the heads of four elephants emerging from the stem. The kangaroo was lost to poachers in the early 1970s and replaced in 1978. The dolphin handles may refer to the City's maritime history or to the famous fishmarket at Billingsgate, the ward of Sir Reginald Hanson, the Lord Mayor responsible for this cup. Like so many of the finest pieces of this period at Mansion House, this was produced by the distinguished firm of Barnard, the successor to Anthony Nelme, Charles Wright, Thomas Chawner and Rebecca Eames. Edward Barnard I passed the firm on to his three sons, Edward II, Charles and William, at his death in 1855. They maintained the firm's reputation for magnificent presentation pieces from their premises in Angel Street, St Martin's Le Grand by St Paul's.

The Jubilee Cup realises the Imperial aspirations of the City and its role in the commercial and political domination by Britain of much of the world by the late nineteenth century. Sir Reginald entertained the Queen to luncheon at the Mansion House on 14 May, accompanied by no less than ten members of her immediate family. A Jubilee ball was also given in June at the House for over 4,000 guests, with eight foreign sovereigns present, including the Queen of Hawaii.

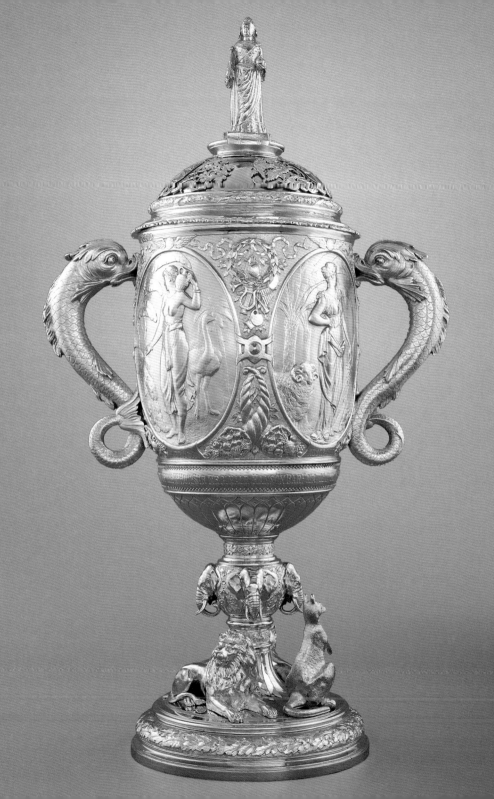

41

The De Keyser Cup and Cover

Bourdon Frères, Ghent, c. 1888
Silver, silver-gilt, enamel, turquoise and cabochon garnets, 54.6 cm high, 2740 gm
Bequeathed by Sir Polydor de Keyser in 1897 (LM 1887–88)

Belgian by birth, Catholic by religion and an hotelier by profession, Sir Polydor de Keyser overcame all these official 'disabilities' to holding high office in the City to become the first Roman Catholic Lord Mayor of London since the Reformation. Alderman for Farringdon Without, he presented his own magnificent cup and cover to the City at the conclusion of his year in 1888 (no. 42).

Sir Polydor's Belgian heritage was of great importance to him and he undertook a State visit to Belgium during his year, when this cup and cover was presented to him by the Belgian government and the municipalities he visited. The eight heraldic lions of the foot bear shields with the arms of the then eight provinces of Belgium. The form of the cup reflects the Late Gothic and slightly severe style of the region – a combination of the bulbous *pokal* form of cup with two layers of lobes and a stepped octagonal foot and lid based on the Low Countries fonts that helped define the cultural heritage of the new Belgian nation during the nineteenth century. The base and the rim of the lid are set with cabochon turquoise and garnets. With eight small *piqué-à-jour* enamel 'windows' in the stem and four enamel shields of the City of London, Belgium and de Keyser surrounding the central knop, considerable colour is achieved. A gilded figure of the Archangel Michael conquering the Devil surmounts the lid, representing guardianship of the True Faith, a not-so-subtle reminder of Sir Polydor's role in England.

The Cup was made in a silver alloy of 900 parts per 1000 by the well-established Ghent silversmiths Bourdon Frères, founded in 1811 by Ferdinand de Bryne and run by three generations of the Bourdon family. Their preference for and command of the neo-Gothic style was instrumental in their being chosen in 1871 to make a papal tiara, a masterpiece of design and technique, as a gift for Pius IX from the ladies of the Belgian court. Armand Bourdon II designed both the tiara and this cup. It was bequeathed in Sir Polydor's will to the Mansion House plate collection at his death in 1897.

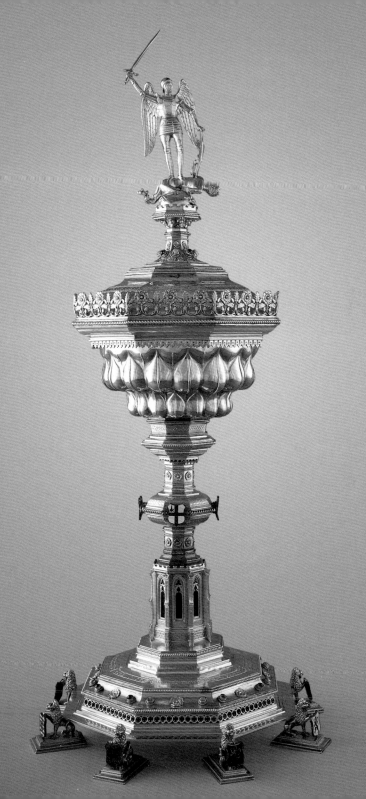

42

The Farringdon Without Cup

Edward Barnard & Sons, London, 1888
Silver-gilt, 45.7 cm high, 2442 gm
Presented by Sir Polydor de Keyser (LM 1887–88)

Born in Belgium, his family originally from Ghent, Polydor de Keyser moved to London in 1845, when he was thirteen. His father founded and ran the highly successful Royal Hotel on the Victoria Embankment at Blackfriars, now the site of Unilever House and formerly of Bridewell Palace. It catered for foreign visitors in particular and only received guests with a written introduction, eventually having rooms for 480 people and 150 staff. Polydor became a member of the Common Council in 1868, an Alderman for Farringdon Without in 1882, Sheriff the following year and Lord Mayor in 1887. A State visit to his native country during his year in office resulted in the presentation of another fine piece of silver, eventually also given to the Mansion House (no. 41).

The present cup and cover, made by the ubiquitous firm of City silversmiths Edward Barnard & Sons, is loaded with symbolism of Sir Polydor's antecedents and achievements. On the lid in three dimensions are the royal arms of Belgium with the Chain of Esses below. Around the rim are the shields of his livery connections – the Spectacle Makers', Loriners', Butchers', Poulterers', Innholders' and Gold and Silver Wyre Drawers' – and his own arms. Below these are four cast and chased distinctive scenes from his ward – Temple Bar, St Paul's with Blackfriar's Bridge, Holborn Viaduct and Snow Hill. Inverted cornucopiae make the handles, while two dragon's wings from the City supporters rise from the stem to the body of the cup.

Edward Barnard & Sons had the distinction of being the oldest silver manufacturing business in London, tracing their history to Anthony Nelme, who started his company in Ave Maria Lane in c. 1680. Passing through the hands of many famous silversmiths, including Charles Wright and Thomas Chawner, the prolific Barnard family gradually took over in the late eighteenth century. From 1838 the firm had their manufacturing premises immediately to the north of St Paul's Cathedral, in Angel Street, where this piece would have been made, moving to Fetter Lane in 1898. The firm closed in 2003.

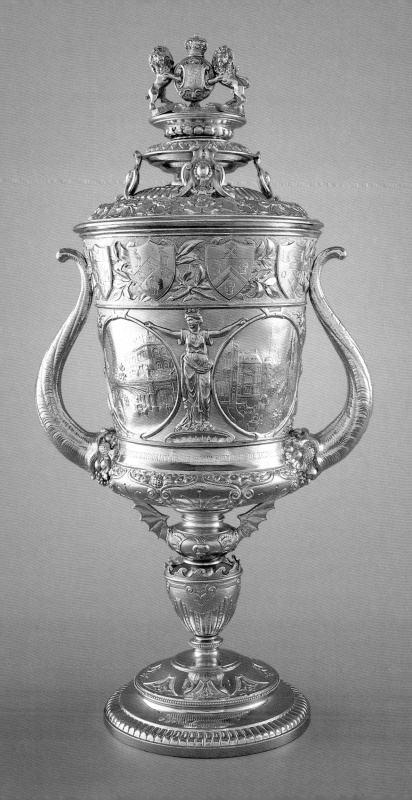

43

The Castle Baynard Cup and Cover

Edward Barnard & Sons, London, 1891–92
Silver-gilt, 48.2 cm high, 2714 gm
Presented by Sir David Evans (LM 1891–92)

Sir David Evans was a Welshman. Born in Llantrisant in Glamorganshire, the young
Evans attended a school at Merton in Surrey before entering the family business of silk
trimmers run by his uncle Sir Richard Evans at Watling Street in the City. He became a
Common Councilman in 1875 and was elected an Alderman for the Ward of Castle Baynard
ten years later. He delighted in his Welsh heritage and spoke the language fluently. He
combined the offices of First Magistrate of the City with that of a Justice of the Peace in
Glamorganshire and led a deputation from the City to his birthplace during his Mayoralty,
being the third Welshman ever to hold the office and the first for seventy years. At a
banquet held at Mansion House for the Welsh of London his four young daughters wore
tall black Welsh steeple hats.

This cup, yet another commissioned from the Barnard brothers (like nos. 37–40, 42, 45
and 48), is laden with symbols of Evans's origins and interests. Four medallions on the
body show Caernarvon, Cardiff and Barnard castles and the Tower of London. Elegant
Welsh harps form the handles, the Principality's three feathers adorn the stem, flanked
by runcible creatures, either Welsh or City dragons. However, Sir David's other great
passion in life rather dominates the iconography (a keen huntsman from his seat at Ewell
in Surrey, he was Master of the Surrey Farmers Hunt) and four stags' heads, riding crops,
hunting caps and horns and a hound surmount the lid.

On the visit to his birthplace in 1892 a choir performed verses penned by Mr Fardo,
postmaster of Cardiff, to the tune of 'God Bless the Prince of Wales', with one verse reading:

> Llantrisant from her mountains
> Smiles o'er Morganwg's vales
> And gives to mighty London
> A real Lord Mayor from Wales.

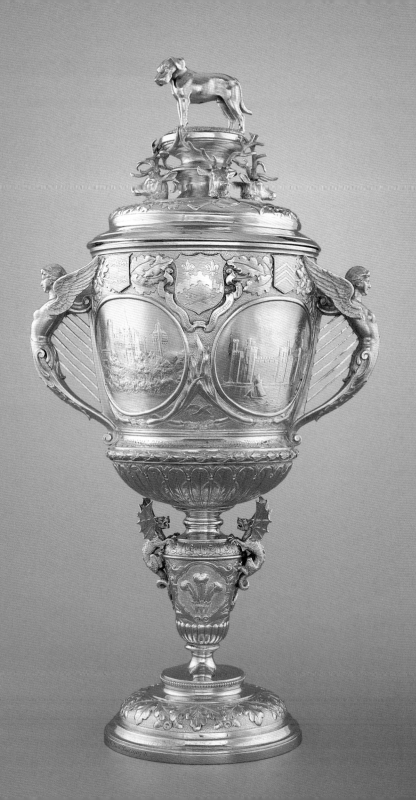

44

The Knill Cups and Covers

(LEFT) Hardman, Powell & Co., Birmingham, 1893–94
Parcel-gilt and enamel, 51 cm high
Presented by Sir Stuart Knill, 1st Bt (LM 1892–93)
(RIGHT) Hardman, Powell & Co., Birmingham, 1910–11
Parcel-gilt and enamel, 55 cm high, 2750 gm gross
Presented Sir John Knill, 3rd Bt (LM 1909–10) in memory of his father

These parcel-gilt cups and covers, differentiated only by the figures on the lids and the enamel shields on the feet, commemorate the father and son Lord Mayors Sir Stuart Knill, 1st Bt, and Sir John Knill, 2nd Bt. Supported by ogee-shaped bases with heavy lobes, the stems are formed of silver flowering rose-briars round a gilt stem. The pear-shaped gilt cups, simple in form and adorned only with inscribed bands on the upper parts, have lids reflecting the lobed feet on which stand figures – on Sir Stuart's St George, his sword raised to strike the dragon, and on Sir John's the winged Archangel St Michael, thrusting a trident into the Devil. Each cup has four enamelled shields at the base of the stem – of the City, the Plumbers' Company, the Goldsmiths' Company and Knill himself.

They were made by the Birmingham firm of Hardman, Powell & Co., leading designers in the Roman Catholic revival of the Gothic style in the later nineteenth century, who worked closely with the famous architect Augustus Welby Pugin on many important commissions, providing stained glass and metalwork to his designs. John Hardman, who founded the firm in 1838, brought his nephew John Hardman Powell into the business. Powell further cemented the relationship with Pugin by marrying his daughter. The Powells' daughter Edith was to marry Sir John Knill, while Sir Stuart Knill's cousin Jane married Pugin as his third wife in 1848. The present cups are a result of this Anglo-Catholic nexus of Pugins, Powells and Knills. Pugin cannot have designed them, however, as he died in 1852, but John Hardman Powell was still active in the business until he died in 1895.

A devout Roman Catholic, a wharfinger and Alderman for Bridge Within, Sir Stuart caused some controversy by declining to enter the City Anglican churches and by proposing a toast to the Holy Father before his toast to the Queen at a banquet he offered to the Catholic hierarchy whilst he was Lord Mayor. The Knill's faith is recorded in these cups by the angelic and saintly figures on the lids, one of the few religious notes in the otherwise staunchly secular Mansion House plate collection.

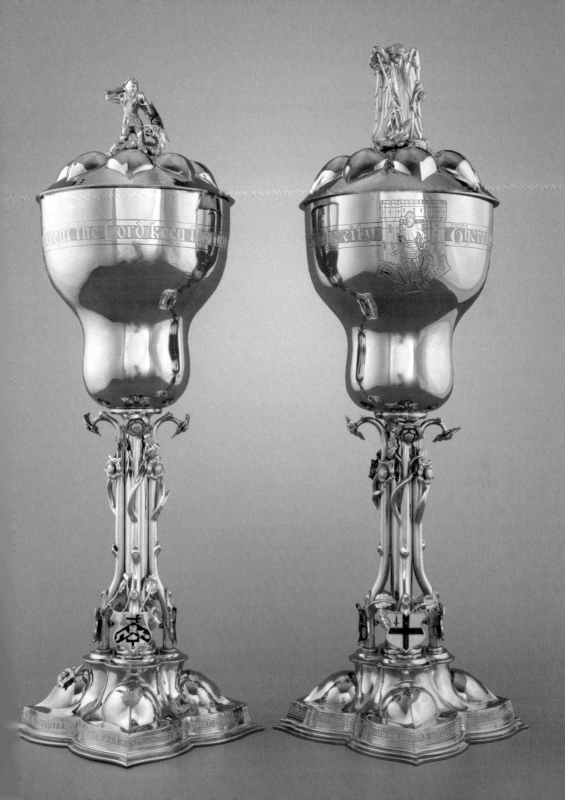

45

The Wilkin Cup and Cover

Edward Barnard & Sons, London, 1896–97
Silver-gilt, enamel and shell cameos, 72.5 cm high, 4221 gm
Presented by Sir Walter Wilkin (LM 1895–96)

Of footed amphora shape, this lidded vase displays all the decorative components of the Greek revival. The form, called a neck amphora, developed from the sixth or fifth century B.C. onwards as a utilitarian and interchangeable vessel for storage of wine and oil into a painted vase for serving or presentation as a prize at feasts and games. The simple tapering body with applied handles that rise above the rim of the neck has been treated to an elaborate but refined application of almost every kind of Greek motif imaginable – the acroterion finial, palmettes, meanderos and anthemions based on the honeysuckle flower. A band of cloisonné enamel enhanced with engraving beneath the subtle translucent colours adds to the richness, and the vase's gilded surface is frosted to give definition to the raised decoration and an antiquarian effect. The enamel band is inspired by classical Greek costume, simple in form but trimmed with embroidered ribbons. Pliny first described these as 'Attalic garments', named after the 2nd century B.C. King of Pergamum, Attalus II, who is credited with the invention of embroidery in gold. The vase was the gift of Sir Walter Wilkin (LM 1895–96), Master of the Broiderers' Company, who had organized a great exhibition of embroidery at Mansion House in 1894. Two cameos, heads of a man and a woman, reinforcing the Greek revival theme, have been set to be removable, allowing the vase to be cleaned without damage to the fragile profiles.

Interest in the colours of the classical world had been growing since Samuel Angell discovered polychromy in Greek architecture in the 1820s. In the 1870s architects like Jacques Ignace Hittorff produced colourful buildings in Greek styles, and in 1878 the Greek textiles collected by the diplomat Humphrey Sandwith were acquired by the South Kensington Museum, further increasing interest. So when Arthur Lasenby Liberty opened his fashionable emporium near Regent Street in 1875, the public demand for classically inspired and colourful fabric was intense. By 1881 Liberty was advertising new designs and hand-made dress accessories, including embroideries from the Near East, Turkey and Greece. With the architect-designer Edward William Godwin, Liberty started a new embroidery workshop in 1884. Among Godwin's designs were what were described as Ancient Greek-pattern trimmings and woven edgings, often in primary colours and utilizing gold thread. Highly successful, Liberty's needle-work may well have influenced the enamellers of the Barnard workshop when required to provide a decorative band to encircle the present vase for the Lord Mayor and Master of the Broiderers' Company in 1896.

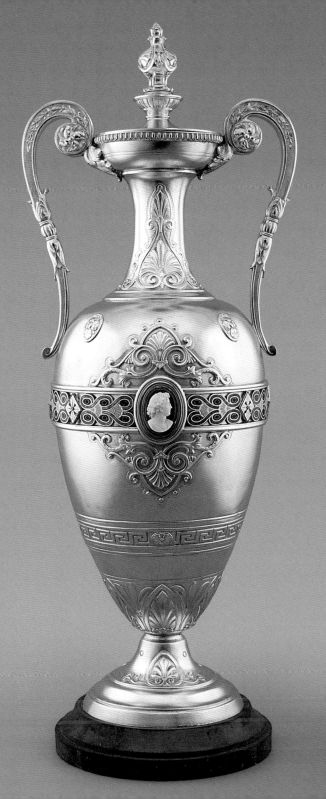

46

The Wells or Olympic Cup and Cover

Walker & Tolhust, London, 1898–99, with later enamel finial *c.* 1948
Silver-gilt and enamel, 38 cm high, 1453 gm
Presented by Sir Frederick Wells, Bt (LM 1947–48)

In the spirit of post-War austerity, Sir Frederick Wells, Lord Mayor during the Olympic
Games of 1948, acquired a late nineteenth-century silver-gilt cup and cover of great
simplicity, to which he had attached the five-coloured enamel brased rings of the Olympic
emblem set in silver. Suitably inscribed about the rim with details of the event and
his position, Sir Frederick's gift to the Mansion House plate collection marks both the
determination to continue the tradition of donations to Mansion House despite the trying
circumstances and the civic pride of London in holding the post-War Games.

London first hosted the Games in 1908, but after the Berlin Games of 1936 none had
been held until those in London in 1948. Fifty-nine nations participated, but Germany
and Japan were barred and the Soviet Union declined the invitation. No new venues
were constructed, nor was there a dedicated village for competitors, of which there were
over 4,000, who gathered at Wembley Stadium for the opening ceremony on 29 July. The
Olympic rings were designed in 1912 by the Games progenitor Baron Pierre de Coubertin.
He said the rings, including the white background, stood for those colours that appeared
on all the national flags that competed in the Olympic Games at the time: "the six colours
thus combined to reproduce the colours of all the nations, with no exception. The blue
and yellow of Sweden, the blue and white of Greece, the tri-colours of France, England
and America, Germany, Belgium, Italy, Hungary, the yellow and red of Spain next to the
novelties of Brazil or Australia, with old Japan and new China. Here is truly
an international symbol."

Sir Frederick was prominent in the ranks of the good and great who took part in the
opening and closing ceremonies. On the night of the opening he hosted a banquet at
Mansion House for the heads of the attending missions. It was unusually lavish thanks to
the generosity of the Lord Mayor of Melbourne, who provided a large quantity of foodstuffs
unavailable in Britain in this time of rationing. It is possible that this cup and cover, with
its simple but significant attachment, might have made its first appearance at Mansion
House at this event.

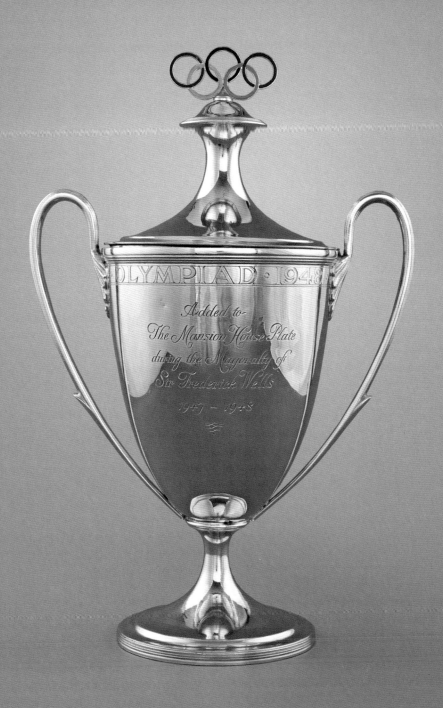

47

The City Cups

46 Elly Isaac Miller & Wilkinson, silver-gilt, London, 1900–01; silver-gilt
6 Jules Golding & Co., London, 1970; silver
1 Richard Hodder & Son, London, 1977–78; silver
1 Wakely & Wheeler, London, 1980–81; silver
1 Hythe Decorative Metal Studios, London, 1981–82; silver
25 M.P. Levene Ltd., London, 2002; silver
2 Wakely & Wheeler, London, 2004–05; silver
2 Wakely & Wheeler, London, 2005–06; silver
Various heights but mostly 12 cm high

The ovoid hemispherical shapes of the upper and lower parts of the majority of these
cups are based on the sherry measures of a schooner (4 oz) and a clipper (2 oz). The initial
group of 46 were given by Sir Alfred Newton, Bt (LM 1899-1900). A remarkably active and
successful man with a great sense of hospitality, Sir Alfred was originally from Hull and in
the shipping business, becoming a director of a large number of commercial firms in the
City and beyond. He also became the chairman of Harrods, the department store, where in
1921 he eventually died, poisoned by strychnine from an unknown hand.

There are cups that are individually assigned to the Aldermen of each of the twenty-five
Wards of the City, and the original set of cups were engraved with the name and dates of
each Alderman. A second set, marked only by each ward name, were intended to replace
them, but the Aldermen did not want to give up their old, named cups, so the second set
are used by their partners. The older cups are now becoming very full of names. There
are also cups for the past Lord Mayors, as well as the Chief Commoner, the Town Clerk,
the Chamberlain, the Swordbearer and the Lord Mayor's Chaplain. There are Sheriff's
cups, though the Aldermanic Sheriff generally uses the Ward goblet, and one for the Lord
Mayor's guest and the Lady Mayoress. That of the Chaplain was presented by the Rt Revd
Gerald Ellison, Bishop of London, in 1981 to commemorate his retirement from that office.
The Common Cryer and Sergeant-at-Arms goblet and that of the City Marshal were added
by the then Swordbearer Brigadier Neill O'Connor in 2005.

Housed in deal, baized-lined boxes that identify the correct cup to the correct office, they
are used at all City banquets at the Mansion House and the Guildhall. The original double
cups may be set either way up.

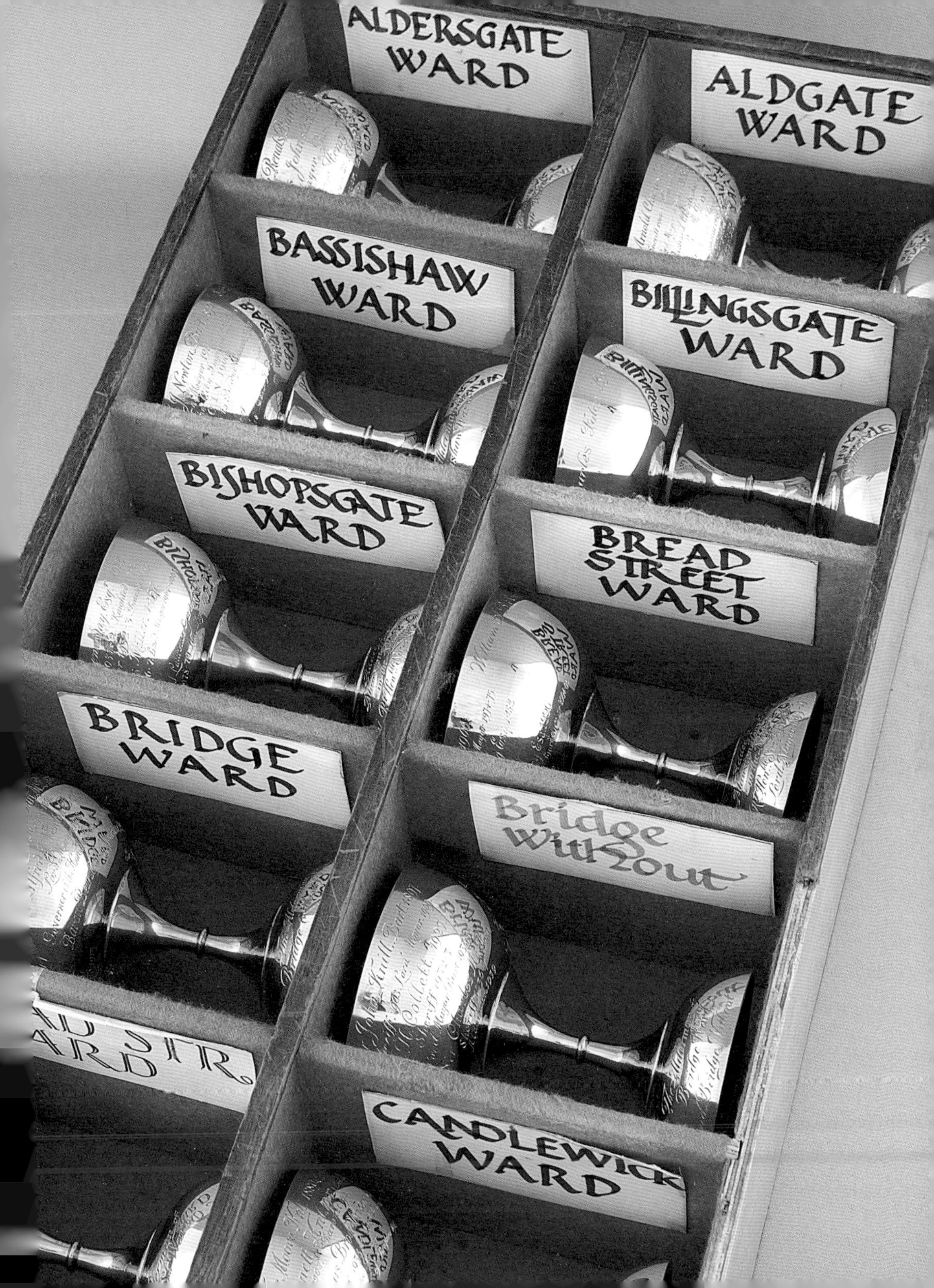

ALDERSGATE WARD

ALDGATE WARD

BASSISHAW WARD

BILLINGSGATE WARD

BISHOPSGATE WARD

BREAD STREET WARD

BRIDGE WARD

Bridge Without

AD STR ARBER

CANDLEWICK WARD

48

The Dimsdale Cup and Cover

Walter, John, Michael and Stanley Barnard and Robert Dubock
for Barnard & Sons Ltd., London, 1902–03
Silver-gilt, rock-crystal and enamel, 46 cm high, 2006 gm
Presented by the Rt Hon. Sir Joseph Dimsdale, Bt, P.C. (LM 1901–02)

Three identical cups were made at the request of the Lord Mayor Sir Joseph Dimsdale to commemorate both his year in office and the coronation of King Edward VII, initially scheduled for June 1902 but postponed until 9 August owing to the King's ill health. Sir Joseph, who was MP for the City as well as Lord Mayor, attended the service at Westminster Abbey carrying the Crystal Sceptre (no. 1), as shown in his portrait at the Guildhall Art Gallery by Arthur Cope. The three cups make an elegant reference to the Sceptre in the tear-shaped crystals mounted in the stems. They were presented to his old school, Eton College, to his livery company, the Grocers, and to the Mansion House.

Besides the unusual insertion of the crystal drop, the body of the cup is pierced with an elaborate lattice and decorated with three enamel shields of the royal arms, the City arms, Sir Joseph's own arms and the crossed Mace and Sword. The technique of piercing an outer sleeve, which allows for considerable virtuosity to be achieved when an inner lining is inserted, is a seventeenth-century conceit but here no insert was added, making the cup impractical. The stem has a decidedly Art Nouveau theme in the violent, whiplash curves of the branches around the crystal, while the pierced rim of the lid, surmounted by the City dragons bearing an Imperial crown, have a decidedly Gothic feel. Despite this apparent stylistic contradiction, the cup is a remarkably fine piece of silver, beautifully crafted, which clearly both delighted the makers and the donor – all the silversmiths responsible applied their mark and an inscription on the foot records that Sir Joseph destroyed all the patterns for the cups afterwards so they could not be repeated.

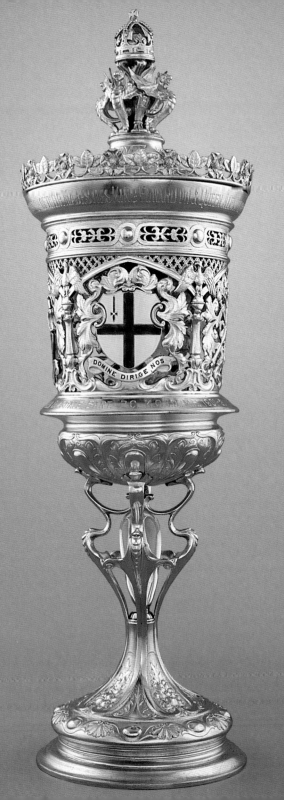

49

The Samuel Cup and Cover

Edward Watherston, London, 1903–04
Silver-gilt, 38 cm high, 3515 gm
Presented by Sir Marcus Samuel, later 1st Viscount Bearstead (LM 1902–03)

The Edwardian Rococo Revival is epitomized by this flamboyant vase and cover of inverted pear-shape with spiral fluting, cast and applied swags of flowers, acanthus and scrolled handles, all magnificently chased, gilded and engraved with the arms of the City and the donor. It also admirably reflects the character of the donor, the rumbustious and exuberant Marcus Samuel, a petroleum entrepreneur. He started his commercial life with a small shop in Shoreditch, selling amongst other items painted shells – hence the name of his company, Shell, which amalgamated with the Royal Dutch Petroleum Co. in 1906. It was nearly fifty years after Sir David Salomons (LM 1855–56) had been elected the first Jewish Lord Mayor of London that Samuel became the second. By virtue of the exertions of Royal Dutch Shell during the Great War, particularly providing fuel and the petroleum distillate trinitrotoluene used to make the high explosive TNT, Samuel was raised to the peerage in 1921.

The West End firm Watherston & Co. were well established in the late nineteenth century as manufacturers and retailers of silver and jewellery, then led by James Watherston and his son Edward, who made this vase. Initially with premises in Pall Mall next door to the National Gallery, their shop was compulsorily purchased as being a fire risk to the Gallery in 1901, when they moved to Vigo Street. They were particularly noted for making replicas of historic silver, but the original model of this vase is unrecorded.

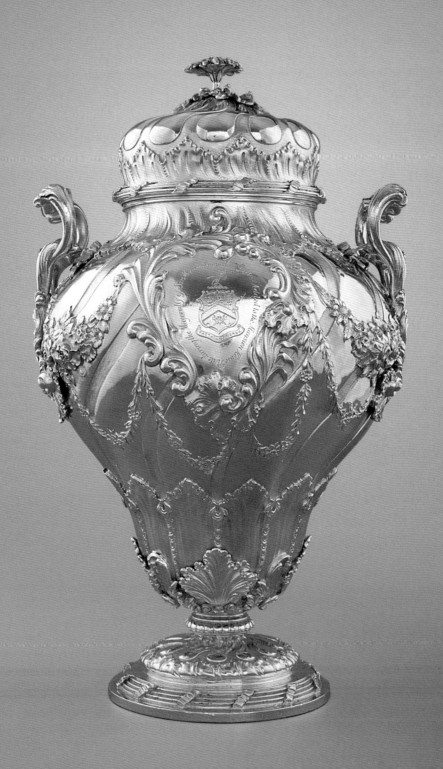

50

The Johnston Cup and Cover

Latino Movio for Johnson, Walker & Tolhurst, London, 1904–05
Silver-gilt, 58.5 cm high, 4883 gm
Presented by Sir Charles Johnston, Bt (LM 1914–15)

This extraordinary cup and cover of comparatively simple, baluster form on a splayed
foot and with small handles rising from the shoulders to join the rim is a masterpiece
of Art Nouveau. The undulating, syncopated rhythms, in this case of a vine-leaf motif,
articulates the bold but plain body of the cup, raised from behind and finely finished.
The influence of modern Japanese work in base metals and silver is also evident. The vine
motif is repeated in the cast stems and leaves of the handles and in the leaves of the lid.
The surface has been deliberately given a spot-hammered finish that emphasizes its hand-
wrought characteristics. It was supplied to the Lord Mayor ten years after its creation
by the fashionable West End firm of Johnson, Walker & Tolhurst for presentation to
Mansion House.

Latino Movio is one of the most enigmatic but distinguished – and, despite never
registering a mark, distinguishable – silver-makers of the period. This is the first of two
magnificent examples of his rare and important work at Mansion House (see no. 56).
Born in Italy in 1858, he was recorded as being from Milan when a piece of his metalwork
won a diploma at the Italian Exhibition held in 1888 at Earl's Court. He appears to have
come to London not before the early 1900s, and worked in the studio of Gilbert Marks.
He was influenced by Mark's sculptural approach to silver and his impressive techniques
of raising and chasing. The mark of LM was assigned to Latino's brother Louis, who had
come to England in the 1890s, teaching raised metalwork in Birmingham, but who died in
1900. Latino worked for retailers, particularly Holland, Ardwinckle & Slater and Johnson,
Walker & Tolhurst, who also sold Gilbert Marks's work. He identified his work by signing
and dating, as on the present cup. Soon falling on hard times, he was advertising his skills
in *The Times* in 1911 saying he would "undertake any situation concerning the art metal
trade". Two of his children followed him into metalworking; his twenty-three-year-old
daughter Theresa Movio is recorded as an art metal teacher in south London in the 1911
census. He died in Belper, Derbyshire, in 1949 aged ninety-one.

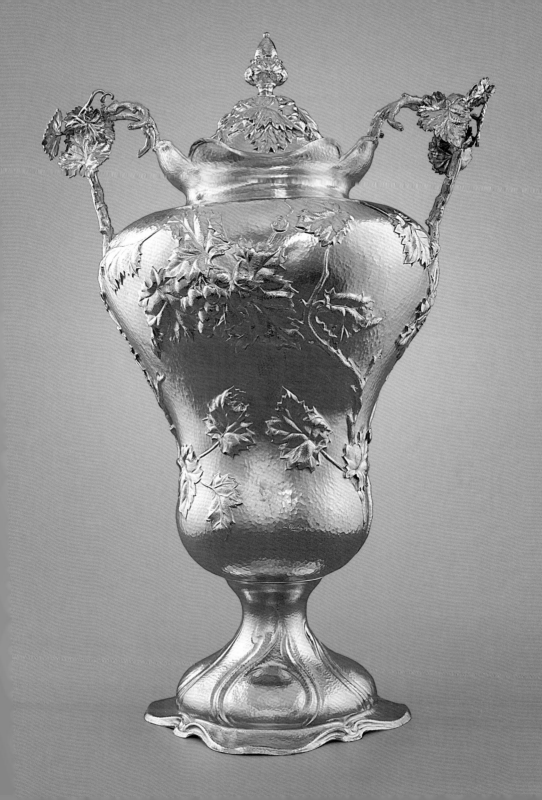

51

The Aldgate Vase

Elkington & Co., Birmingham, 1905–06
Silver-gilt, 31.7 cm high, 5739 gm
Presented by Sir John Pound, Bt (LM 1904–05)

The tapering ovoid form of this footed vase, with vine-scroll handles rising from the high shoulders, is loosely based on the ancient Greek form of either a *stamnos* or a *hydria*, both intended for the storage and serving of liquids. The burnished undecorated surface of the body highlights the cast and chased decoration, which, combined with the inset medallions on either side, refer to the theme of hospitality – in this case that of Sir John Pound during his Mayoralty. The vase is named after the ward Sir John represented as an Alderman.

The wheat-ears and vines, symbolizing bread and wine, invoke the several State and official events over which the Lord Mayor presided in the year 1904–05, including Sir John's own State Banquet on 10 November 1904, commemorated in the large medallion on the front. The back of the vase shows oval relief portraits of the royal and republican guests of the City. The year got off to a good start, and a week after the State Banquet a luncheon was held at the Guildhall for King Carlos and Queen Amélie of Portugal, who were accompanied by the Prince and Princess of Wales. On 5 May 1905 the Lord Mayor and Corporation entertained the outgoing American ambassador Joseph Hodges Choate to a farewell banquet at Mansion House. King Alphonso XIII of Spain was entertained at the Guildhall on 7 June during his State Visit to Edward VII and Queen Alexandra. Prince and Princess Arisugawa Takehito, returning to Japan through London from the marriage of the German Crown Prince in Berlin, were entertained to luncheon at Mansion House on 30 July. Finally, 10 August 1905 marked a banquet in honour of Admiral Leonce Caillard, Chief of Staff of the French Navy, whose Channel Squadron was on a visit to Cowes during the Regatta week. He and his staff were entertained by the King at Windsor and by Parliament at Westminster Hall as well as by the Lord Mayor at Mansion House, celebrating the Entente Cordiale.

It is slightly strange that Sir John commissioned the vase from the Birmingham firm of Elkington rather than from a company closer to home. However, considering the close connection between Elkington and the eminent sculptor and medallist Sir George Frampton R.A., it is possible that Frampton provided the medallions for this vase.

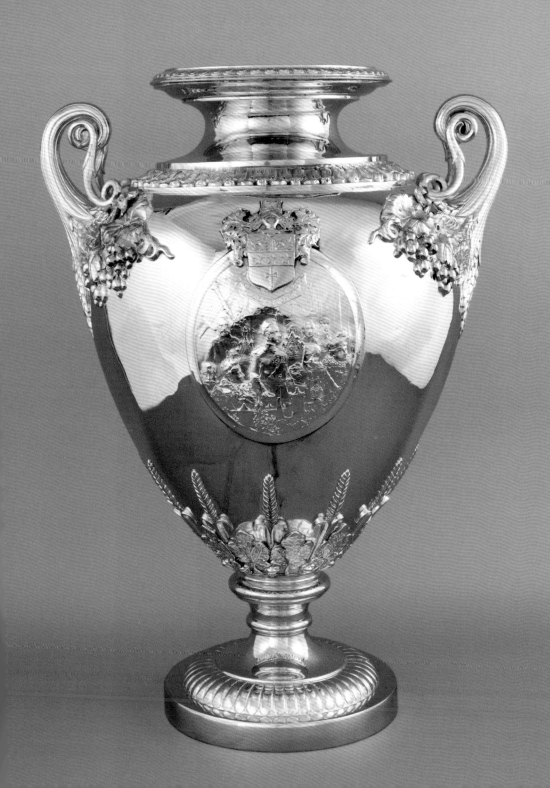

52

Two Warwick Vases

Daniel & John Wellby, London, 1906–07
Silver-gilt, 29.8 cm, 7434 gm
Presented by Sir John Bell (LM 1907–08)

Edward Barnard & Sons Ltd., London, 1918–19
Silver-gilt, 48.2 cm high, 8106 gm
Presented by Sir Robert Tasker, Chairman of London County Council, 1930–31

These two examples of the Warwick Vase are differentiated only by the slightly taller foot of the later version. The original Warwick Vase, now in the Burrell Collection, Glasgow, is a monumental Imperial Roman marble vase, some 178 cm high, dating from the reign of the Emperor Hadrian. It was excavated in many fragments from a lake at Hadrian's villa near Tivoli in 1770 and extensively restored, indeed effectively completely rebuilt on a new marble body. Acquired by the 2nd Earl of Warwick from his uncle Sir William Hamilton by 1778, it stood for many years at Warwick Castle before being bought by the Burrell in 1979.

Engraved by Piranesi soon after its restoration, the vase became one of the most influential and copied of all classical antiquities. The Bacchic iconography of masks and Priapic staves notwithstanding, the rectangular base, the shallow *katharos* form, bold gadroons beneath the bowl and entwined vine handles that spread under the egg-and-dart rim became common forms in decorative arts in the early years of the nineteenth century. As Lord Warwick initially refused to allow the vase to be copied, Piranesi's prints became the source of the model by Paul Storr around 1811 for Rundell, Bridge & Rundell, copied endlessly by English silversmiths throughout the nineteenth century. Used primarily as a wine-cooler or simply as a centrepiece, the Warwick Vase is also known in the functions of soup or sauce tureens, racing trophies, salts, jardinieres and even a tea service, by Robert Hennell II of 1821. The two present examples, without liners, are purely decorative.

The first example was presented by Sir John Bell, a wealthy brewer and Master of the Fan Makers' Company, who was instrumental in reviving the Lord Mayor's Show as a popular pageant. He bought it from Wellby's, a jewellery and silver retailer then in Garrick Street. The actual maker is unknown, though Edward Barnard & Sons, makers of the second example, often supplied Wellby's with high-quality silver. The company produced models of the Warwick Vase in silver and silver-gilt in a variety of sizes, including miniature replicas. As Eames & Barnard, they had been making models of the vase since at least 1821. The second example was acquired, ten years after it was made, by Sir Robert Tasker, who served as Chairman of London County Council in 1930–31. He presented it in that year to the Mansion House plate collection "as a token of [his] veneration and affection for the City", reflecting the strong relationship between the Corporation and the rest of London that still exists.

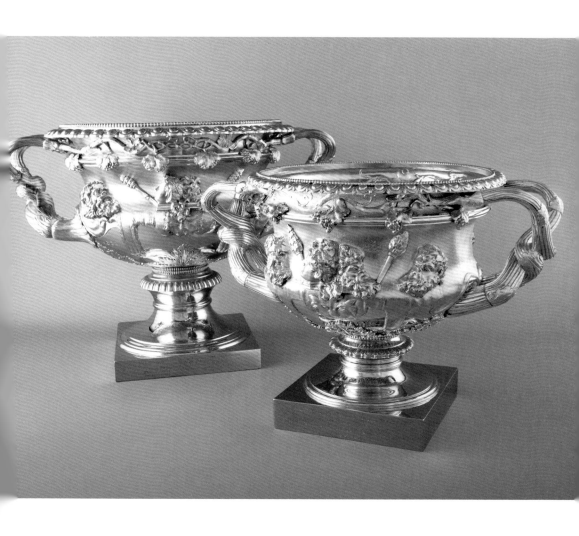

53

The Christ's Hospital Cup and Cover

Goldsmiths & Silversmiths Co. Ltd, London, 1906–07
Silver-gilt, 62.8 cm high, 5163 gm
Presented by Sir Walter Vaughan Morgan, Bt (LM 1905–06)

The high, bell-shaped foot of this large cup rises through a flattened baluster to a swagged vase on which rests an open cage of four foliated term figures that support the broad but shallow incurvate body of the bowl. Two thin scrolled handles rise from the broadest part of the body to the rim, while the low, stepped lid supports the figure of a Christ's Hospitalier in his traditional uniform. Four plaques in low relief decorate the body, divided by the handles and cast and chased arms, those of the City on one side and those of the donor, Sir Walter Vaughan Morgan, on the other.

The iconography of several of the late nineteenth and early twentieth-century pieces of silver in the Mansion House collection is hard to decipher, and this cup is no exception. Its complex imagery highlights various disconnected elements of the donor's private, charitable and public lives. Vaughan Morgan came from Glasbury-on-Wye in Powys, the sixth of nine sons of a successful wool stapler. His father handled almost all the wool from Wales until 1839, when, facing bankruptcy, he sought and obtained for Walter and another son presentations to Christ's Hospital, then in Newgate Street in the City. The boys, once grown, prospered, eventually founding the firm of Morgan Brothers, merchants and bankers, with three more of their siblings. Walter maintained his connection with the 'Bluecoat school', becoming a governor in 1873 and then Treasurer of the Council of Almoners in 1891, a position he held during his Mayoral year. He used any occasion to promote the welfare of the school, mercilessly using his connections and particularly his friendship with the Prince of Wales, later George V, who had become President of Christ's Hospital in 1904 upon the death of his uncle, the Duke of Cambridge. The Duke and Vaughan Morgan had seen off the attempts of the Charity Commissioners to change the Hospital's status but they had agreed to the new building for the boy's school at Horsham, for which the foundation stone was laid in 1897. The Lord Mayor presided at the opening of the newly rebuilt girls' school at Hertford during his year. The name, the finial figure and the view of the old Great Hall recall these aspects of his life.

Sir Walter's trade missions to the Universal Exhibitions in Milan and Paris in 1906 are reflected in the view of Milan Cathedral on the cup, and the State Banquet for his inauguration is represented in another scene. Through The Irish Society the Lord Mayor was friends with William Gibson, one of the founders of the Goldsmiths & Silversmiths Co. Ltd, which exhibited and won medals at both Universal Exhibitions, and were therefore a natural choice for the commission of this cup.

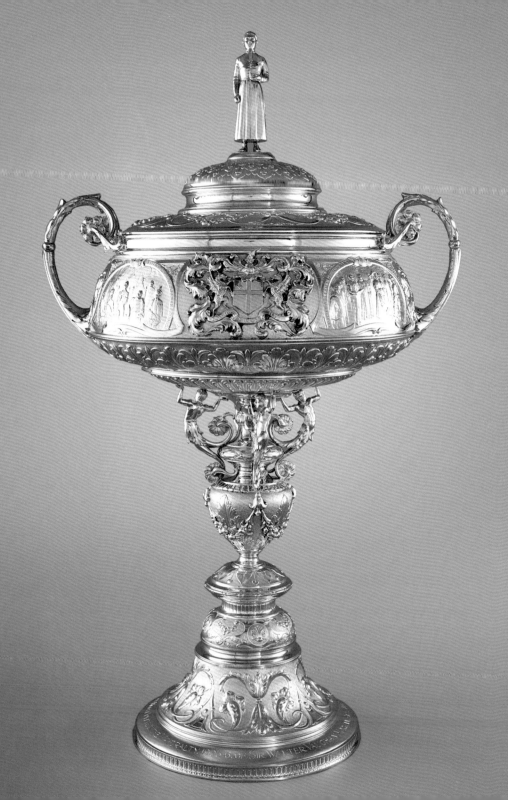

54

The Treloar Cup

Elkington & Co., Birmingham, 1906–07
Gold, 18-ct, enamel and semi-precious stones, 19.7 cm high, 762 gm
Presented by the London Central Markets to Sir William Treloar, Bt (LM 1906–07)
and bequeathed by him to the Mansion House plate collection in 1923

This delightful Art Nouveau-style cup is made of a deep red gold, set with cabochon semi-
precious stones – tourmaline, garnet and topaz – with the City arms in three dimensions
and coloured enamel within the stem. The auricular base of sinuous lobes supports
three inwardly scrolling C-shaped brackets. These in turn support the drum-shaped cup,
which is embossed with a lengthy inscription in stylized uncial script that records the
circumstances of its creation and presentation.

The large and famous firm of Elkington, run by several generations of the Birmingham-
based family, had opened premises in London in 1893, in Cheapside, and it is from there
that the commission for this cup would have been made, though the hallmarks reveal it
was made in Birmingham. Elkington, most famous for their mastery of the techniques of
copying silver in alloy, improved their design workshops in the late nineteenth century by
employing a number of skilled French designers who brought the latest Parisian fashions
to the firm. This cup must be the work of one of these talented but anonymous designers.

Lord Mayor Treloar recorded in his diary the events of 9 November 1906, when he was
carried to the Law Courts to be sworn in as Lord Mayor: "My carriage stopped in the Central
Markets, where an address in a beautifully bound album containing the names of the
subscribers was presented to me by Mr William Cooper on behalf of the Market tenants
of the Corporation. A splendid gold loving cup, specially designed and manufactured by
Elkington, accompanied the album. I drank from the cup that same evening at Guildhall
to some of my friends." The commissioners of this highly aesthetic and ultra-fashionable
piece of gold were an unlikely group – the tenants of the Central London Markets, better
known as Smithfield, comprising mostly butchers and poulterers. Their landlord was the
City of London.

Treloar was Alderman for the Ward of Farringdon Without, known for housing "the
world, the flesh and the Devil" – the newspapers of Fleet Street, the meat of Smithfield and
the lawyers of Temple. Treloar founded what eventually became the Treloar Trust, which
now runs one of Britain's most important specialist centres for the education and training
of young people with physical disabilities, including the Treloar School and College at
Alton in Hampshire. The Lord Mayor of London is now automatically a trustee during
his year.

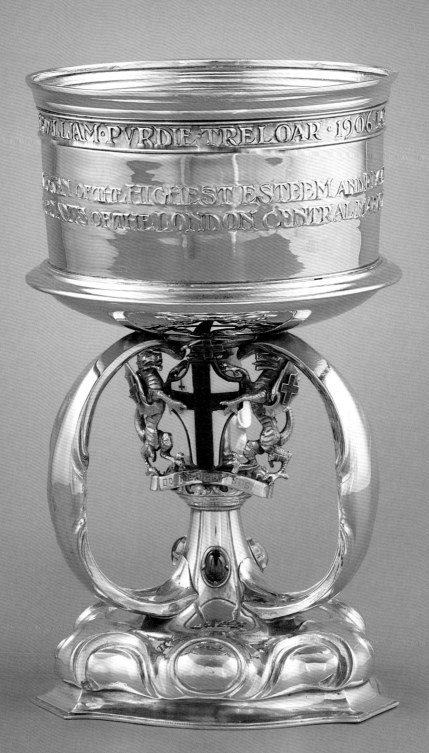

55

A model of the Mace of Tower Ward

W.J. Carroll, London, 1907–08
Silver-gilt, 47.6 cm high, 3710 gm
Presented by Sir James Ritchie, Bt (LM 1903–04)

The original silver model of the White Tower at the Tower of London on which the
present work is based was made in 1671 as the head of the mace of Tower Ward. The four
sides of the tower were engraved with the royal arms of Charles II, the City arms, the
figure of Justice and lastly a dedicatory inscription, giving the date of 20 June 1671 for its
presentation to the ward. Further inscriptions record repairs and alterations in 1677, 1726
and 1772. Four indented flags bearing the King's cypher fly from crowned poles on the
corner turrets, while the figure of a soldier stands on the roof with four cannons. This
replica of the upper third of the mace is life-size and accurate in all details. It was made by
Walter James Carroll, who is listed primarily as a watchmaker, a local to the Tower at Beer
Lane, Great Tower Street.

The model was presented to Mansion House by Sir James Ritchie during his Mayoral
year. A wealthy jute merchant, he had been Alderman for Tower Ward since 1891. His
younger brother, an MP for the City, was successively Home Secretary and Chancellor
of the Exchequer in Conservative ministries, and Sir James tried but failed to enter
Parliament himself. He was a popular Lord Mayor, however, and greatly mourned when
he died in 1912.

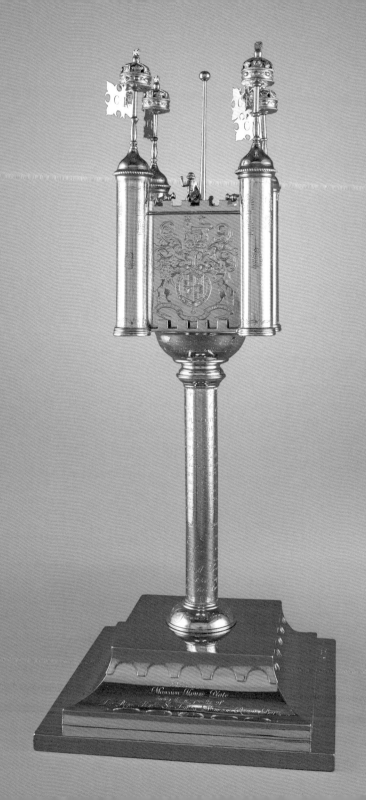

56

A rosewater dish

Latino Movio for Holland, Aldwinckle & Slater, London, 1908–09
Silver-gilt, Britannia standard, 58.4 cm diameter, 4432 gm
Presented by Sir George Truscott, Bt (LM 1908–09)

This spectacular dish is one of the most exciting and important pieces of silver at
Mansion House. The roses, tendrils, bees and butterflies are raised in high, almost three-
dimensional relief from the reverse, a laborious and painstaking procedure that must have
taken many months. The theme of water and roses reflect the ancient use to which the
form of these dishes were put, but largely abandoned by the early twentieth century.
Ovid was clearly right to extoll the great worth of things with no actual utility!

The Art Nouveau design has been influenced by contemporary Japanese metalwork,
particularly the finely matted finish of the swirling lobes, thousands of tiny hammer
marks creating a rippling, delicate surface in contrast to the massive solidity of the dish
overall. Movio, who never registered a maker's mark, completely vanished as a metalworker
soon after this piece was made – he died in 1949, forgotten. A second piece by him, the
Johnston Cup of 1904–05 (no. 50), is also at Mansion House. He signed this piece in minute,
spidery letters deep amongst the rose leaves. The dish captures perfectly the *Zeitgeist* of the
Edwardian age – richly luxurious, slightly provocative and a contrast to the grandeur and
pomposity of the recent Victorian era.

What induced Sir George Truscott to choose this remarkable piece of silver for
presentation to Mansion House is a mystery, but the City should be thankful. Son of a
previous Lord Mayor, he was a Stationer and ran a successful City printing firm for many
years, showing no signs of being a heteroclite in his civic or private life. The delicate
inscriptions recording the City arms and Sir George's, along with a dedication, blend
admirably into the watery roundel in the centre.

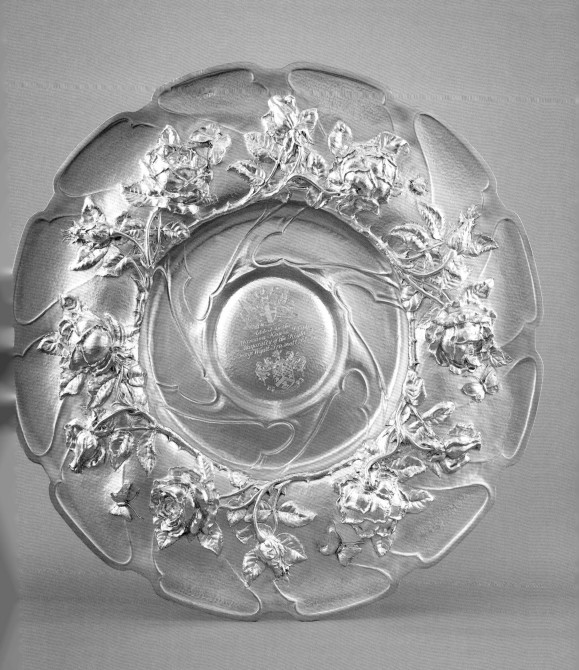

57

An inkstand

Elkington & Co., Birmingham, 1908–09
Silver and enamel, 36.8 cm wide, 36.8 cm high, 7340 gm
Presented by Sir William Treloar (LM 1906–07)

The pieces of regalia and silver associated with Sir William Treloar are of the greatest interest and highest quality. Standing on a plateau with eight stepped feet and containing two inkwells and pen trays is a scale model of Temple Bar. Originally marking the barrier into the Liberties of the City on the western side between the Strand and Fleet Street, the gate was named after the Temple Church and Inns of Court on the southern side of the street. It marks the spot where sovereigns most frequently enter the City, stopping to ask permission, symbolically receiving and returning the Pearl Sword (see no. 4) to the Lord Mayor as they do so. During the improvements to London undertaken after the Great Fire, a new gate was built, probably to the design of Sir Christopher Wren, recording the restoration of the House of Stuart, being paid for by the King, whose statue along with that of his father Charles I stand in niches on one side with those of his grandparents James I and Anne of Denmark on the other.

Charles Dickens described the gate as "that leaden-headed old obstruction, appropriate ornament for the threshold of a leaden-headed old corporation". Treloar had expressed great interest in the fate of the Temple Bar and in 1875 he had proposed in Common Council that it be re-erected in Battersea Park, a motion that was not carried. It was eventually removed in 1878 to ease the flow of traffic, and the City had its 2700 stones carefully stored. In his *Diary* Treloar noted "I shall never cease to regret that this beautiful historic monument was thereby lost to London". His affection for it continued into his Mayoral year, when Waring & Gillows made a replica of it around the doorway into the Egyptian Hall as the entrance to the Queen's Fête, held to raise funds for Treloar's crippled children's fund, which Queen Alexandra opened with a golden key on 13 June 1907. In 1880 the brewer Henry Meux, at the insistence of his wife, had bought the stones and re-erected the Temple Bar as a gatehouse in Theobald's Park in Hertfordshire, and it stayed there in a woodland until 2003. In 1938 Theobald's Park was bought, but not the Temple Bar, which remained the property of the Meux Trustees and was later sold to the Temple Bar Trust for £1. In 2001 the City of London resolved to fund its return to the City, and it was rebuilt in Paternoster Square beside St Paul's Cathedral in 2004 at a total cost of £3 million.

This inkstand usually sits on the Lord Mayor's desk in the Venetian Parlour at Mansion House.

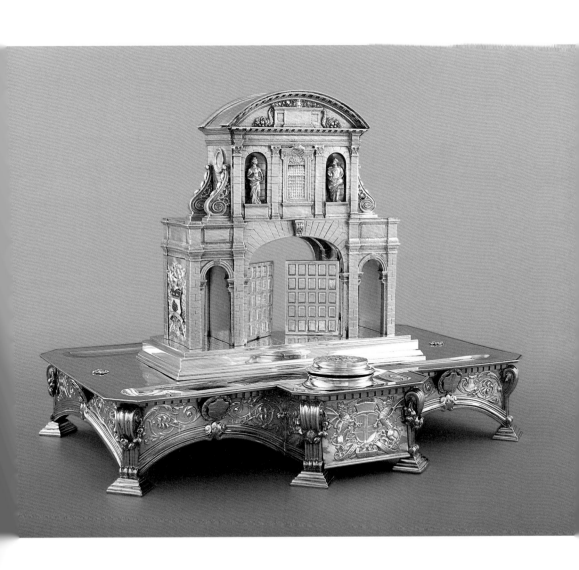

58

A model of the Coronation Chair

Joseph Rogers & Son, Sheffield, 1913–14
Silver-gilt, silver and sandstone, 26.7 cm wide, 19 cm deep, 56.5 cm high, 9207 gm
Presented by the Rt Hon. Sir Thomas Strong, P.C. (LM 1910–11)

Stead's Review in 1911 described Lord Mayor Strong as having "an imagination which is stimulated instead of being crushed by the mass of historical relics with which a Lord Mayor is encompassed". Sir Thomas carried the most important City relic, the Crystal Sceptre (no. 1), at the coronation of King George V on 22 June 1911. He also commissioned this silver replica of the Coronation Chair, which took three years to make. The original, still housed in Westminster Abbey and sometimes called 'St Edward's Chair', was ordered from one Master Walter in 1297 by Edward I at a cost of 100 shillings. The four carved and gilded lions on which it rests were added in the sixteenth century and replaced in 1727. It was made specifically to hold the 'Stone of Scone', reputedly Jacob's pillow when he dreamt of the ladder to Heaven. Captured by King Edward from the Scots in 1296, the Stone was returned to Scotland in 1996 but is due to be returned for future coronations.

The heavy and disfiguring graffiti on the back of the original throne are here 'covered' by a silver sheet inscribed with a speech delivered by King George V at a Guildhall banquet on the 29 June 1911, a few days after the coronation. The hall was decorated with all the Mansion House plate and many treasures from the livery companies. The King concluded his address by saying, "I beg you to believe me, my Lord Mayor, that I shall strive by every means in my power to preserve the prosperity and pre-eminence of my capital city". Dame Clara Butt then sang the national anthem. A further lengthy inscription on the seat records the commission from Sir Thomas, who was made a Privy Councillor. The block of sandstone, cut to replicate the Stone of Scone, is even set with two iron rings, as is the original.

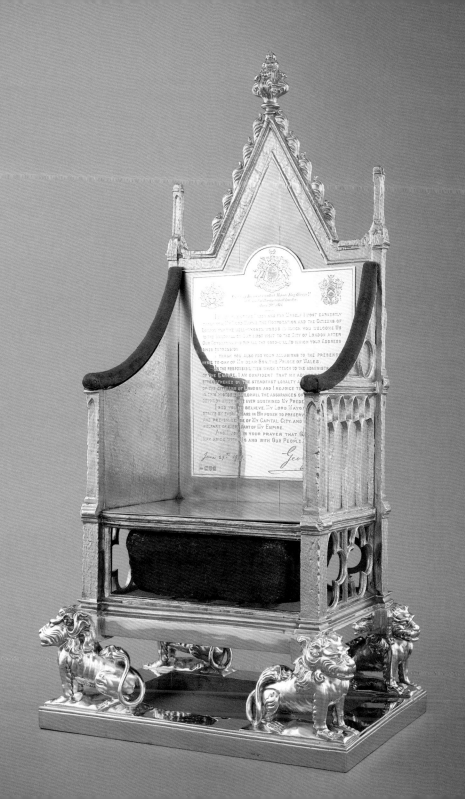

59

The Wakefield Cup and Cover

Charles Stuart Harris & Sons, London, 1911–12
Silver-gilt, 73.5 cm, 7278 gm
Presented by Sir Charles Wakefield, Bt (LM 1915–16), later Viscount Wakefield of Hythe

Despite its late eighteeth-century design, this elegant cup and cover was made by the firm of Harris & Co., probably as an item for stock, in 1911–12. The high ribbed acanthus handles and the bat-wing fluting on the foot, the lower body and lid are all drawn from the severe Neoclassicism of late eighteenth century. The frieze around the upper body is cast and chased with scrolls and roundels of classical scenes of Diana the Huntress. The Cup was then embellished with three later medallion scenes, an inscription and the engraved arms of the City and the donor, which modestly commemorate the circumstance of the gift to the Mansion House plate collection at the height of the First World War.

Charles Wakefield, a proud Liverpudlian, entered the lubricant oil business at a very early date, setting up business in London in the 1890s and developing his own brand called Castrol, named after the fragrant castor oil it contained. Success followed in the tracks of motorcars, motorcycles and eventually aeroplanes. Sir Charles – he was knighted in 1908 – led recruitment drives during the Great War with his close friend Lord Kitchener, as recorded here. The medallions show a reception for new soldiers at Mansion House, where Wakefield stood from 8 am until 8 pm welcoming each recruit personally, the scene after a service at St Paul's, and a visit Wakefield made to the Western Front in 1916 that was then followed by a visit to the Fleet at Scapa Flow. Sir Charles was described as having an "unusually well-developed sense of obligation to the state as a guardian of society".

The invention by Castrol of an aeroplane engine oil that did not freeze in the low temperatures at high altitudes gave the Royal Flying Corps a significant advantage over Germany during the War. It also brought Wakefield a considerable fortune, which was used for many good causes, including the Guildhall Art Gallery and funding the acquisition for the nation of, amongst other objects, the Armada Jewel, Isaac Newton's papers and the Codex Sinaiticus for the British Library. He also bought the Brass Crosby Cup for the Mansion House plate collection in 1935 (no. 18).

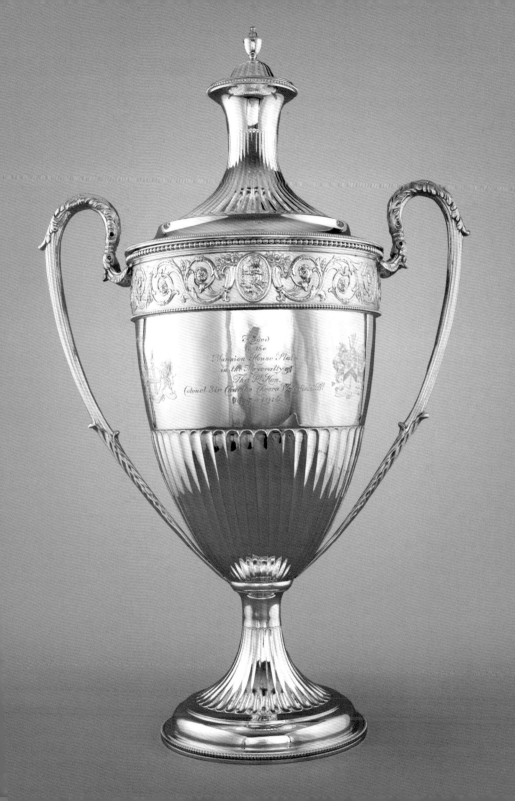

60

The Bowater Jardiniere

Johnson, Walker & Tolhurst, London, 1914–15
Silver-gilt and enamel, 49 cm long, 25.4 cm wide, 27.3 cm high, 5536 gm
Presented by Sir Thomas Bowater, Bt (LM 1913–14)

Of exuberant design, filled with optimism for an early victory for the Allies in the War with
Germany just begun, this handsome jardiniere would become by 1918 a hollow memorial
to jingoism, false hopes in false dawns. Standing on massive hairy paws, the scrolled base
has lion masks on either side, the British Lion of heroic actions and unfettered pride. The
heads of the King George V and Queen Mary take up the patriotic theme under the scrolls
at either end. In the centre of each side is an enamelled arrangement of the Allied flags,
with Britain and France in the centre, flanked by what nowadays might seem strange
neighbours – Russia, Japan, Holland and Belgium. The neo-Rococo form was well suited to
the soon-to-pass Belle Époque of peace, progress and prosperity. Few would have dreamt
in these early years of war what horrors were to come and at what cost victory would be
achieved.

   At the outbreak of war on 4 August 1914, Lord Mayor Sir Thomas Vansittart Bowater
had just returned from an official visits to Paris in June and Brussels in July, where not
three weeks before he had been entertained by Adolphe Max, the Mayor of Brussels, to a
State banquet, and where the City deputation had dined with King Albert I and Queen
Elizabeth. Max was imprisoned by the Germans for the entire war. The rest of Bowater's
Mayoralty was taken up with the war effort, recruiting battalions for the City of London
regiment and raising funds. His four sons all served in the forces during the war and all
survived. His gift of silver to the Mansion House plate collection reflects his concern for his
new friends and the rightness of the Allied cause.

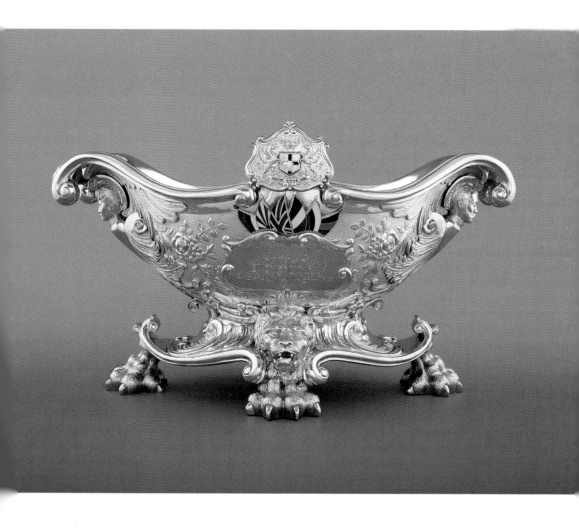

61

An inkstand

Atkin Brothers, Sheffield, 1914–15
Silver-gilt and glass, 45.7 cm long, 30 cm wide, 4666 gm
Presented by Sir David Burnett, Bt (LM 1912–13)

This unusual inkstand, standing on four scroll feet supporting a gadrooned plateau, records three of the outstanding events of the Mayoral year of Sir David Burnett. A chartered surveyor who gave his entire working life to the benefit of the City, Burnett had been instrumental in saving the Crystal Palace from extinction, raising funds for its purchase with *The Times*. Built to house the Great Exhibition in Hyde Park in 1851, to the design of Joseph Paxton, the vast steel and glass exhibition hall was disassembled and rebuilt at Sydenham in 1854. Following a slow decline and faced with bankruptcy, it was bought by the 1st Earl of Plymouth, from whom Sir David's trust purchased it for the nation. Greatly altered in the rebuilding and by subsequent use, it finally burnt to the ground in 1936. The model on the inkstand shows it in its altered form, with added transepts and towers. Two oval medallions at the front corners record other notable events from Sir David's year, one showing the mining disaster at Senghennydd in South Wales on 14 October 1913, when an underground gas explosion killed 440 men, the worst mining disaster in British history. The Lord Mayor's fund raised over £75,000 for the victims' families. The second shows Sir David in Common Council with Lady Burnett beside him during his election to the Mayoralty in 1912.

Atkin Brothers was one of the oldest – and largest – of the Sheffield manufacturing silversmiths, and had, like many similar firms outside London, an office in the capital to facilitate orders and commissions from their global clientele. Charterhouse Street, by Holborn, is where Sir David's commission for this inkstand would have been received for manufacture at Atkin Brothers' Truro Workshop in Matilda Street, Sheffield.

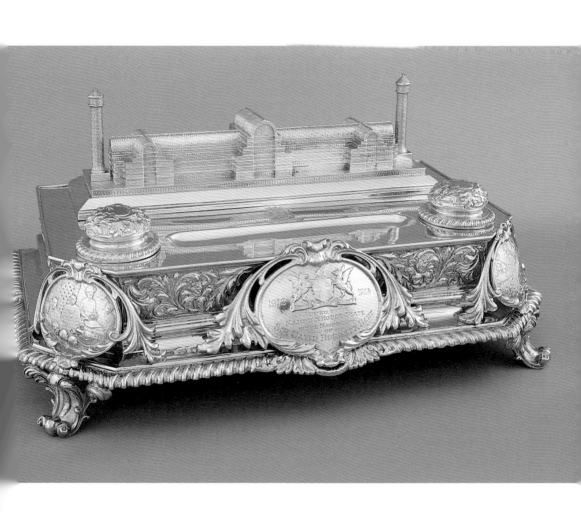

62

A model of The Great Harry

Charles & Richard Comyns, London, 1919–20
Silver-gilt, 49.5 cm, 2768 gm
Presented by Sir Frank Alexander, Bt (LM 1944–45)

Sir Frank Alexander, chairman of the Baltic Exchange and Prime Warden of the
Shipwrights' Company, was a ship-broker and ship-owner. He was also chairman of
Capper, Alexander & Co., a shipping line founded in Cardiff in 1875 which lost all its ships
to enemy action during the Second World War. Elected Lord Mayor at the end of hostilities,
Sir Frank gave the City a model of the flagship of the Tudor fleet – a poignant reminder of
the losses as well as the gains of war.

   The Tudor flagship was *Henry Grace à Dieu*, commonly called 'The Great Harry', built
at Woolwich between 1512 and 1514 and named for King Henry VIII. The first English
two-decker, the Great Harry was originally fitted with 43 heavy and 141 light guns at 1,500
tons burthen. Top-heavy and unmanageable, she was refitted in 1535 at Erith, at the same
time as the *Mary Rose*. Reduced in height and now with only 21 heavy guns, she was 1,000
tons burthen. This model is an accurate reproduction of the remodelled ship, based on
the Anthony Roll in the Pepys Library at Magdalene College, Cambridge (Ms Pepys 2991),
an illustrated inventory of the English fleet completed in 1546 by Anthony Anthony for
Henry VIII. The ship saw little action, though she did carry the King to France in 1520 for
the meeting with François I at the Field of the Cloth of Gold. She is believed to have died in
the 1550s.

   The makers of the model, Charles and Richard Comyns, owned a large silver
manufactory business in Soho, founded in the 1850s by their father but incorporating an
older, probably eighteenth-century business with origins in the firm of Rundell, Bridge
& Rundell. In 1923 they advertised specializing in "reproductions from the Antique".
The model is largely machine-made, from silver plates cut and soldered; only the finer
details of the cannon, rigging and carved stern were cast and chased. The base of mahogany
is set with plaques engraved with the arms of Sir Frank Alexander and the City, recording
the donation. Several other examples of this model are known in silver, made by the
same maker.

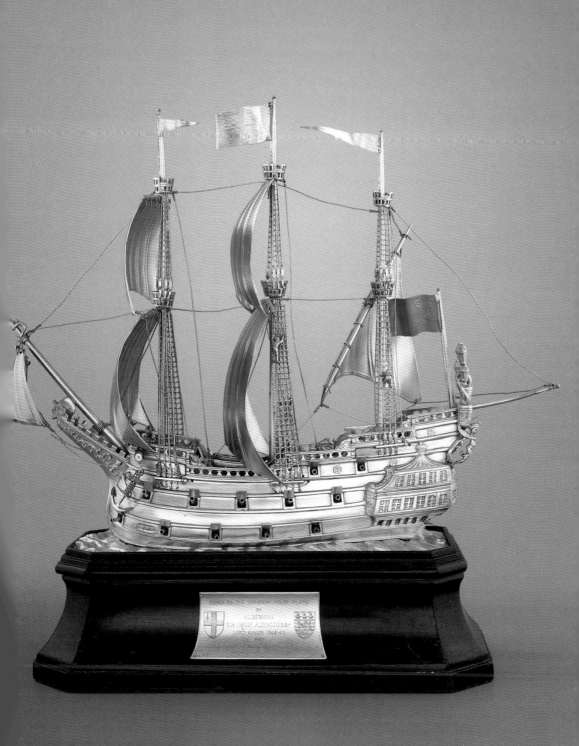

ADDED TO THE MANSION HOUSE PLATE
BY
ALDERMAN
SIR FRANK ALEXANDER Bt
LORD MAYOR 1944-45
AND

63

The Marshall Cup and Cover

Jay & Attenborough, London, 1920–21
Silver-gilt, 57 cm high, 3145 gm
Presented by the Rt Hon. Sir Horace Brooks Marshall, P.C.
(LM 1918–19), later Lord Marshall of Chipstead

The end of the First World War is symbolized by the figure of Peace carrying a wreath of laurel on the lid of this cup, presented by Sir Horace Brooks Marshall, who was elected Lord Mayor in November 1918. His year was almost completely taken up by the events, celebrations and thanksgivings that surrounded the end of the Great War. It was at his State banquet at Guildhall on the evening of 9 November that the Prime Minister presented the thrilling news of the abdication of the Kaiser, leaving "that potent empire that threatened civilization hapless and headless". The Lord Mayor announced the Armistice from the portico of Mansion House the following Monday to scenes of unbridled joy. Freedom of the City was presented by Sir Horace to many of the victors during his year, including Lords Beatty, Haig and Allenby, President Wilson, General Pershing, Marshal Foch and the Shah of Persia.

Of a traditional form on a trumpet-shaped foot and tapered body, the cup is engraved with the arms of the City on the front and those of Sir Horace on the back. The gilding has worn on the balusters of the stem, where it has been handled over the years. The foot is further engraved with the details of the designer, the sculptor of the figure of Peace and the engraver.

Designed by a young Oliver Hill, later to become better known as an architect and architectural gardener, the etiolated stemmed foot is rather uncomfortable on a piece of secular silver. Gilbert Bayes was already a distinguished sculptor, but the demand in the 1920s for figurative war memorials enhanced his reputation, eventually leading to his presidency of the Royal Society of Sculptors. The elegant calligraphy is by Phillip Rainger, of whom nothing is known, and the marks are those of an undistinguished firm of jobbing manufacturers incorporating a large pawnbrokers, based in Oxford Street.

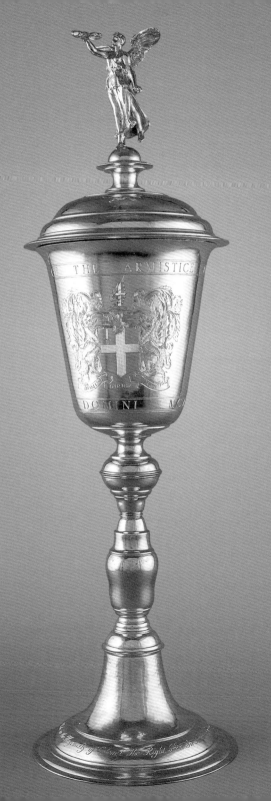

64

A cigar casket

Alexander Clark Manufacturing Co., London, 1921–22
Silver-gilt, cedar-wood and enamel, 41.2 cm long, 15.2 cm wide, 24 cm high, 3748 gm
Presented by Sir James Roll, Bt (LM 1920–21)

No trace remains of the original parcel-gilding, presumably removed by wear and heavy weather over the years. The broad, moulded base supports a long box with a cedar-lined drawer, the front of which bears the cast and chased arms of the City in enamel. The handles, backed by tridents and anchors, are semicircular leaf and berry swags that frame two painted enamel roundels showing scenes from the several manifestations of Billingsgate Fish Market. Its collection of sheds and open arcaded buildings were demolished in 1850 for James Bunstone Bunning's building, which quickly gave way in 1877 to Sir Horace Jones's grandiloquent, neo-Italian palace, which still stands but was eventually itself superseded when the fish market was moved to the Isle of Dogs in 1982. On the top of the box is a scale model of the kind of steam-and-sail coastal trawler, common in the Thames and North Sea in the late nineteenth century, that brought fish to the Billingsgate wharf, just above the Tower of London. Part of the ship's bridge is a cigar cutter, the funnel acted as a lighter and ventilators at either end are cigar piercers.

Needless to say, Sir James Roll was Alderman for the Ward of Billingsgate. Chairman of the Pearl Assurance Company, he was also fond of driving, being a member of the Worshipful Company of Carmen and owned a coach for many years. He was an enthusiastic member of the Pickwick Club, where members referred to each other by their Dickensian names at meets and even State occasions, Sir James being 'Mr Pickwick' himself. That Sir James regarded a magnificent cigar box – rather than an impractical piece of great presence but little use – as an appropriate gift to the Mansion House plate collection was a sign that entertainment and the pleasures of the table were becoming the focus of events at Mansion House.

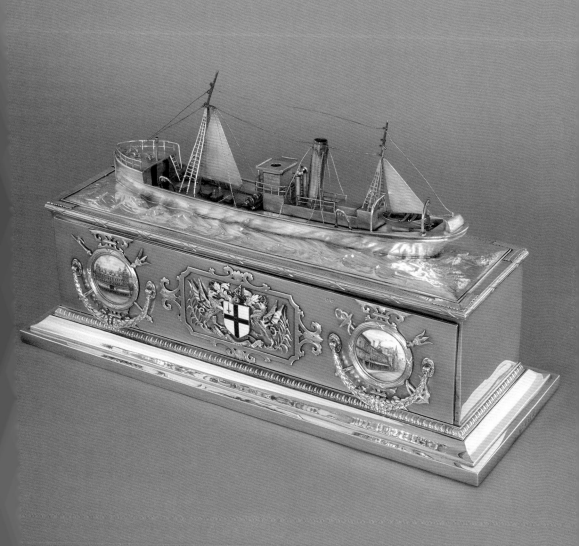

65

The Batho Salt-cellars

William Hutton & Sons Ltd., Sheffield, 1928–29
Silver-gilt and glass, 11.5 cm high, 9 cm diameter, 4082 gm gross
Presented by Sir Charles Batho, Bt (LM 1927–28)

These eight salt-cellars are amongst the earliest pieces of twentieth-century silver at
Mansion House that reflect the changes of taste and style from the long nineteenth
century and Edwardian period towards some form of modernism. Standing on simple,
circular and slightly domed bases, the plain shafts have an industrial feel of cogs and
pistons, supporting the circular moulded drums with semispherical glass-lined receptacles
for the salt. The design is enhanced and enlivened by the four cast dragons emerging from
the shafts, their scales finely chased. They grip the rims of the flanged ring mouldings,
mouths wide open and tongues protruding, appearing in somewhat comical fur hats –
these reproduce the hat of the Lord Mayor's Swordbearer, which sometimes replaces the
visored helm in the arms of the City. In these dragons, reminiscent of the eagle-headed
gargoyles that decorate the famous 1928 Chrysler Building in New York, echoes of the
current Art Deco style are loudly heard and are of exactly its date.

The salts bear the arms of Batho on the foot. Sir Charles was a worthy if unexciting
Lord Mayor, a partner in Copland & Co., ships store and export merchants, called
unexpectedly early to the chair when the original candidate withdrew. A member of the
Paviors' Company and the Gardeners and Basketmakers, he was also a member of the
Baltic Exchange. As a child on his way to school in Highgate, he had regularly passed
the Whittington milestone, from which came his determination to become Lord Mayor,
the success of which ambition is happily recorded by these remarkable salt-cellars.

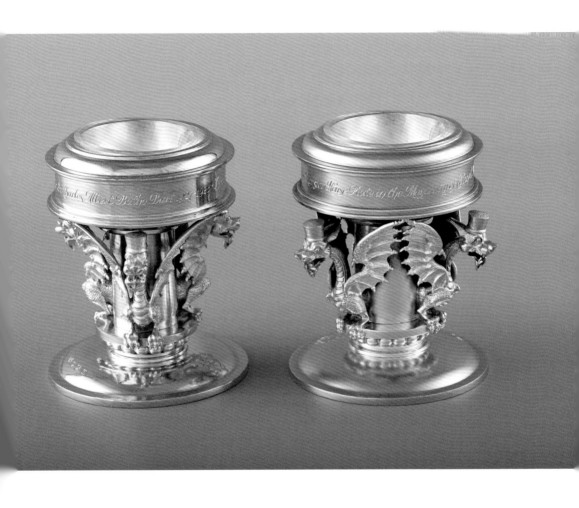

66

A tazza

Omar Ramsden, London, 1931–32
Silver-gilt, 47 cm diameter, 32 cm high, 5723 gm
Presented by Sir William Waterlow, Bt (LM 1929-30)

It is often difficult to determine why a Lord Mayor went to a particular silversmith to commission a commemoration of his year. This spectacular piece of silver-gilt by one of the most outstanding determinists of the later period of the Arts and Crafts movement, Omar Ramsden, is therefore exceptional in that we know that the Lord Mayor who presented it, Sir William Waterlow, was himself given a tall silver vase and cover made by the same maker at his installation on 9 November 1929. A gift from the London Master Printers' Association, of which Sir William was a past president, it too was decorated with grapes and vine leaves. Sir William is known to have owned a number of other pieces by Ramsden and was a knowledgeable patron and client. Waterlow & Sons, of which Sir William was chairman, were printers of currency, postage stamps and stock and bond certificates. His great-uncle Sir Sydney Waterlow had been Lord Mayor in 1872-73.

Ramsden's design of a footed shallow dish is fairly conventional in form, though the wavy rim and the neo-Gothic decoration of the junction of the foot and the stem are typical of his style. Following the dissolution of his near twenty-year partnership with Alwyn Carr in 1919, Ramsden had sole proprietorship of the workshop at St Dunstan's in Seymour Walk, just off the Fulham Road. He fulfilled outstanding commissions, on behalf of livery companies and an affluent corporate clientele including the Lord Mayor: his large pair of vases presented by Lord Mayor Greenaway (no. 69) are notable for their scale as well as their craftsmanship.

In the present piece the combination and juxtaposition of styles conflict to defy all design logic, resulting in a highly tactile masculine object, enhanced by an extravagant use of raw materials bordering on excess. Ramsden has visited several centuries of the design palette: the medieval rising foot is surmounted with Gothic mouldings beneath a castellated rim, and a brutally rigid Art Deco cast fruiting-vine calyx sits below the fluid Art Nouveau bowl. This pastiche of periods melded together received two further treatments before completion: the entire surface was spot hammered to produce Ramsden's signature 'hand-wrought' finish and was then exquisitely gilt using the mercurial method – a dangerous technique, now banned. It is chased and engraved:
I WAS WROUGHT FOR USE IN THE MANSION HOUSE OF THE CITY OF LONDON BY COMMAND OF WILLIAM ALFRED WATERLOW KBE TO MARK HIS YEAR OF OFFICE AS LORD MAYOR 1929–1930.

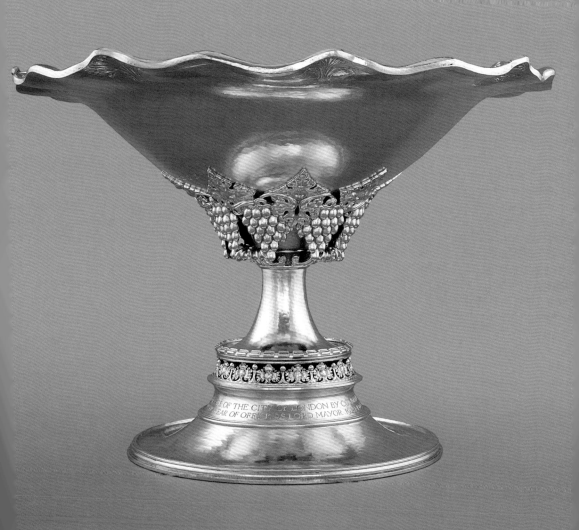

67

The Collett Cup and Cover

Mappin & Webb, London, 1935–36
Silver-gilt, 55.8 cm high, 4012 gm
Presented by Sir Charles Collett, Bt (LM 1933–34)

The form of a double-handled cup and cover, standing on a circular foot, with a tall body
and conical lid is a well-established trope in silver, here re-interpreted in the Art Deco style
ultra-fashionable in the mid 1930s. The creation of this cup has a sad and poignant history.
Sir Charles Collett, in the retail hosiery trade and a member of the Glovers' Company, came
originally from Suffolk. His second son, Stanley Collett, had joined the Royal Flying Corps
during the Great War and flew with Commander 'Bomber' Harris on hundreds of missions
over enemy territory. After the War he became a successful lawyer but returned to the
Auxiliary Air Force in 1925 and rose to the rank of Squadron Leader by 1933, when his father
became Lord Mayor. In July the following year he was killed in an Empire Air Day display
at Hendon, crashing his bi-plane on take-off. He was honoured with a funeral in St Paul's
Cathedral. Sir Charles bravely continued as best he could, but ill health dogged his final
months in office and he quietly retired to Southwold in November 1935, dying three years
later.

The design can be attributed to the New Zealander Keith Murray, who designed
ceramics for Wedgwood in the late 1920s and worked as a freelance designer for Mappin &
Webb in the 1930s. Furthermore he had served with distinction in the Royal Flying Corps
during the First World War and may well have known Stanley Collett. This cup captures
the *Zeitgeist* of the 1930s – a bold new design for a bold new type of defence in the form of
the Royal Air Force, whose crest of an eagle, wings outstretched, stands on a terrestrial
globe on the lid. The R.A.F. motto of *Per Ardua ad Astra* (Through adversity to the stars) is a
poignant reminder of the sacrifices, in many forms, that Lord Mayors have made for their
City and their country over the centuries.

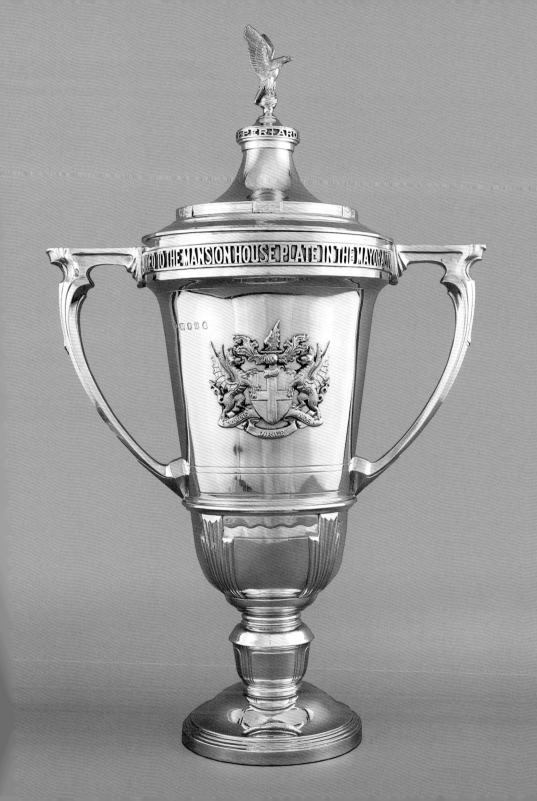

68

A pair of beakers and covers

Wakely & Wheeler for the Goldsmiths & Silversmiths Co. Ltd, London, 1935–36
Silver-gilt and mother-of-pearl, 35.5 cm high, 2448 gm gross
Presented by the Worshipful Company of Goldsmiths, 1935

These stylish beakers and covers in silver-gilt with faceted mother-of-pearl knops were
presented to the Mansion House plate collection in 1935 by the Worshipful Company of
Goldsmiths to commemorate the Silver Jubilee of King George V, who had succeeded to
the throne on 6 May 1910. Standing on simple ring-moulded feet, the tapered bodies are
strongly engraved with figures of addorsed mermaids in two registers, their fluid tails and
arms entwined, alternately facing forwards and backwards, upwards and downwards. The
ripple effect of the engraving is reflected in the wavy moulded rims and mother-of-pearl
knops. The beakers reflect the fashion for Art Deco *streamline moderne*, with their simple
outline, geometric knop and the clean, economic lines of the engraved design.

They were designed by Reginald Gleadowe, who had studied at the Slade School of
Art before becoming a naval officer during the First World War and then an assistant
to the Director of the National Gallery. In 1923 he became Head of Art at his old school,
Winchester College, where he remained for the rest of his life; he was also Slade Professor
of Art at Oxford from 1928 to 1933. He was an active designer of decorative arts, making the
famous Sword of Stalingrad during the Second World War as a gift from King George VI to
honour the Russian resistance to German invasion.

The engraving is the work of George Friend, who taught engraving at the Central School
of Design until the late 1960s. A friend of Gleadowe's, he had collaborated with him on
an earlier piece, the Sea Beaker of 1933–34 now in the Victoria and Albert Museum, with
similar mermaids, waves and fishes. Why these motifs were chosen to celebrate the Jubilee
is unclear. Made by Wakely & Wheeler on behalf of the Goldsmiths & Silversmiths Co.
Ltd, they bear the Jubilee hallmark for 1935. Sir Stephen Killik was Lord Mayor during the
Jubilee and with the Aldermen and Common Council entertained the King and Queen at
Guildhall to a banquet a fortnight after the anniversary. Killik presented his own piece –
an eighteenth-century silver-gilt cup and cover, suitably inscribed – to the Mansion House
plate collection (no. 20).

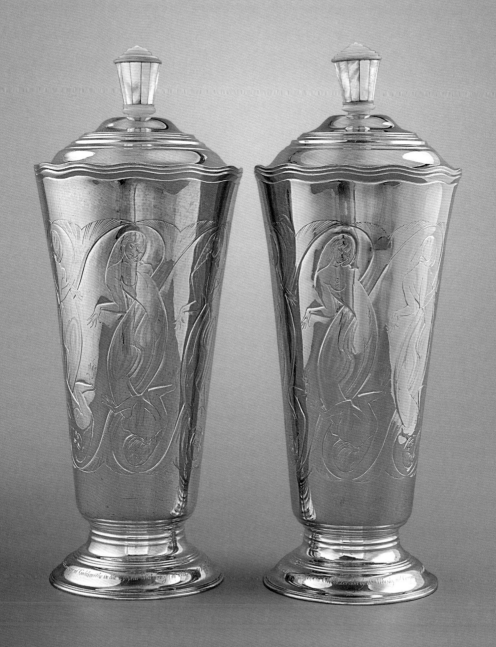

69

A pair of vases

Omar Ramsden, London, 1936–37
Silver-gilt, 63 cm high, 8398 gm gross
Presented by Sir Percy Greenaway, Bt (LM 1932–33)

The iconography of these vases is aquatic – female nudes cavort in the waves on the bases, which rise through lily-pads and reeds to open in rippling waves at the top that finally open out into almost full-blown bowls. There is nothing, however, to link the theme to the thoroughly respectable and staid Lord Mayor Greenaway. A stationer and printer by trade, he devoted over forty years to service in the City, first as a member of the Court of Common Council from 1917, then Alderman for Bishopsgate and finally as Lord Mayor. He may well have been aware of Ramsden as a silversmith from the tazza presented by Sir William Waterlow in 1931 (no. 66), but the four-year delay between the end of his Mayoralty and the completion of these vases supports the evidence of the inscription that this was a commission rather than the purchase of pieces already made.

Ramsden, however, unceremoniously raided the parts-bin in his Fulham workshop to fulfil the order. The dramatic figural bases are cast from an earlier pattern used for a pair of candlesticks, the columns making way for the tall trumpet-shaped receptacles. He used the model again in the centre of a bowl with a similar aquatic theme in 1935. The Art Deco marine elements of the bases are almost static, while the freer, swirling, fluted upper sections impart movement. The problems involved in combining different elements and periods is not without risk: the awkwardness of height and form of these vases provides a challenge for even the most expert florist.

The bases are chased and engraved: *I WAS WROUGHT FOR THE MANSION HOUSE BY THE COMMAND OF SIR PERCY WALTER GREENAWAY BARONET ALDERMAN OF THE WARD OF BISHOPSGATE TO MARK HIS YEAR OF OFFICE AS LORD MAYOR 1932–33.*

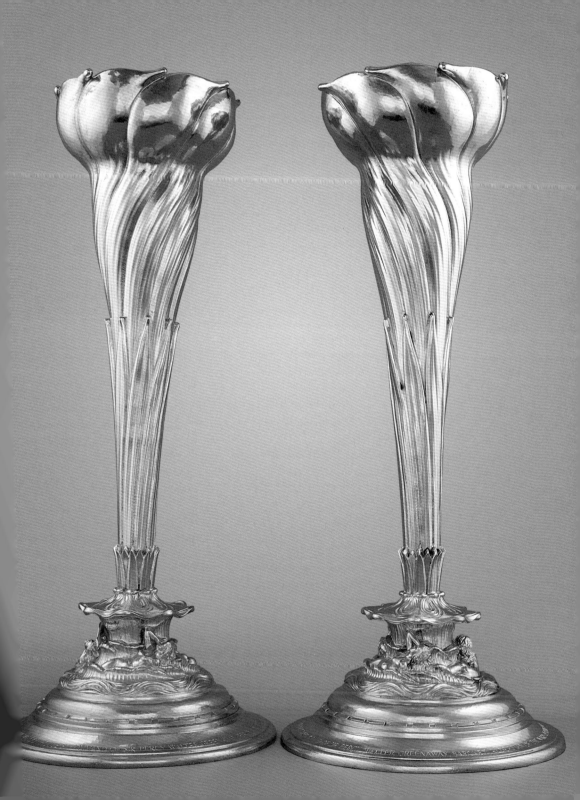

70

The Vincent Cup and Cover

Hinklenton & Phillips, London, 1936–37
Gold, 9-ct, and alabaster, 16.5 cm high, 513 gm
Presented by Sir Percy Vincent, Bt (LM 1935–36)

This solid gold cup and cover is a replica of a treasure of Exeter College, Oxford, made in the 1660s and presented to the college by an alumnus, George Hall, Bishop of Chester, at his death in 1668. Hall was a fellow of the college and a famous pluralist, holding several other valuable offices: he was canon at Windsor, vicar of Wigan in Lancashire and chaplain to King Charles II. Hall died when he fell off a mound in his garden, impaling himself on a pocketknife.

The original cup is unmarked but is inscribed with the donor's name and the name of the college, which are left off the copy. The lozenge-shaped lobes are decorated with scrolls and strapwork, while the larger lobes on the body about the rim are engraved with realistic flowers and leaves of a viola type. It is one of the few Caroline pieces of gold to survive, showing much influence from Continental work, particularly German makers of the mid century. Floral decoration, either engraved or in repoussé, was also very popular in this decade. Arthur Mainwairing or Nicolas Woolaston are possible makers for the original cup and cover. An electrogram copy in the Victorian and Albert Museum may have served as the model for this copy, rather than the original in Oxford. It was made by Hicklenton & Phillips, a manufacturing and retail firm that had been founded in 1910 by two former employees of Mappin & Webb, with premises in Cheapside and Cannon Street by the 1930s – conveniently close to Mansion House. It stands on a pristine white alabaster plinth with a gold plaque giving notice of the donation to the Mansion House plate collection.

Mansion House's tenant in 1936 was Sir Percy Vincent, who had left home at the age of thirteen to work in the textile business, opening his own warehouse in his mid 1920s. He is not known to have had any connection with Oxford, so must have chosen this gold cup and cover simply for its aesthetic pleasure. He was the first Lord Mayor to visit North America on official business during his year and took with him all his ceremonial robes and regalia of office, and even wanted to take the eighteenth century golden State coach, which was considered too delicate to travel. He presented the City of Vancouver with a replica of the City Mace (see no. 7), made from Canadian silver by the Goldsmiths & Silversmiths Co. Ltd.

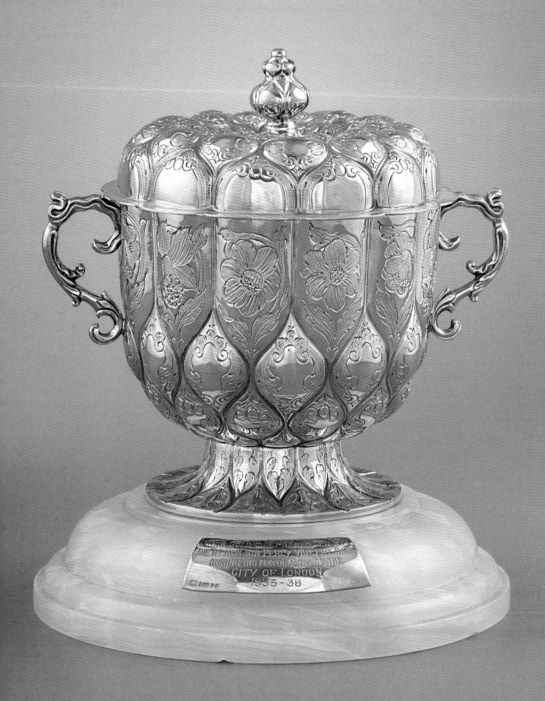

THE R'T HON. SIR PERCY VINCENT BART
DURING HIS MAYORALTY OF THE
CITY OF LONDON
1935-36

71

A cigarette box

Deakin & Francis, Birmingham, 1945
Gold, 9-ct, enamel and an approx. 5-ct diamond, cedar lined, 12.7 cm high,
20.3 cm long, 1170 gm
Presented by the Diamond Manufacturers Association of London, 1945

London has often offered safe haven for persecuted minorities. In 1656, when, for doctrinal
and practical reasons, Oliver Cromwell received the Jewish community from Holland.
Whether Huguenots in the seventeenth and eighteenth centuries, displaced nobility
during the French Revolution, starving Irish labour during the nineteenth-century
famines or Jewish refugees fleeing tsarist pogroms in eastern Europe in the late nineteenth
century, London has constantly given diasporas a home and a living. Before and during the
Second World War, the City yet again opened her arms to welcome refugees from Europe,
as this magnificent diamond-set gold box can testify. Presented at the end of the war by the
Diamond Manufacturers' Association of London, the box has an inscription on the front
that records their "appreciation of the hospitality which many of them, who are refugees,
have enjoyed in Great Britain since the occupation by the enemy of their homelands".
Many former residents of Antwerp, engaged in the diamond trade and of Jewish origin,
escaped to Britain; 15,000 were reported, though many skilled sorters and cutters later
made their way either to New York or to Palestine.

The flared sarcophagus form, standing on four stepped feet that rise to flanged brackets
on each corner, is deceptively simple. The curved short ends of the lid, coupled with
the bracketed feet and quatrefoil and diamond-set knop, give discreet direction to the
declining Art Deco style. Even the elegant font of the moving dedication is reflective of
the times, while the materials speak not only of the occupations of the donors, but of their
thankfulness at their rescue and of the spirit of the age in art. The beautifully cast, chased
and enamelled arms of the City, combining silver and gilt with the *argent* and *gules* of the
heraldry, add restrained richness. Though of a significant weight, the large diamond set in
silver exhibits small occlusions, as is to be expected in a stone of this size.

There is very little silver in the Mansion House plate collection from the late 1940s and
1950s, largely owing to the very high Purchase Tax of the time, which almost ensured
that precious metal objects were not produced. The Design and Research Centre set up at
Goldsmiths Hall in 1945 nonetheless administered an 'Assistance to Craftsmen Scheme',
which introduced tax relief for pieces "entirely hand-wrought" that displayed "excellence
and workmanship". A fear that modernity would be unpalatable to the general public
meant conservatism in the silver trade. A large number of reproduction Georgian pieces
were made and the styles of the 1930s and 1940s revived – hence the distinctly dated feel of
this box.

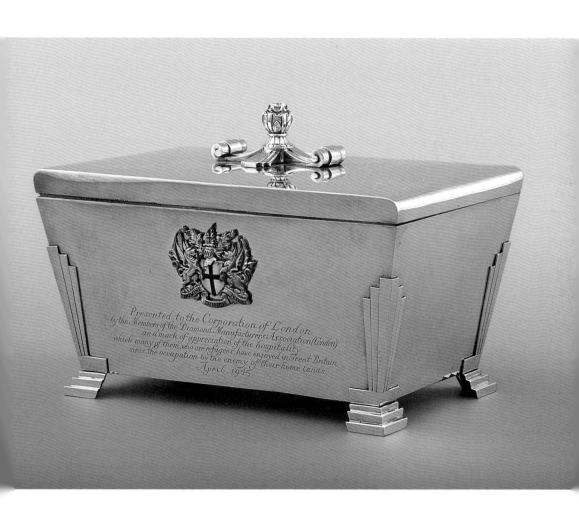

Presented to the Corporation of London
by the Members of the Diamond Manufacturers Association (London)
as a mark of appreciation of the hospitality
which many of them, who are refugees, have enjoyed in Great Britain
since the occupation by the enemy of their home lands.
April, 1945.

72

A footed salver

Mappin & Webb, Sheffield, 1946
18-ct gold and enamel, 42 cm long, 32 cm wide, 2053 gm
Presented by the City of Johannesburg, 1948

This oval salver standing on four small scrolled legs was a gift from the City of
Johannesburg, economic capital of South Africa, to the City of London in 1948. It was
presented to Sir Frederick Wells (LM 1947–48) at a ceremony at Mansion House on
22 January by the South African High Commissioner, Leif Egeland. Inscribed in English
and Afrikaans it records the *appreciation of the great part played by the people of Britain and
London in particular in the cause of freedom and justice during the Second World War*. With Tudor
roses and South African proteas at either end and within the border, the scalloped edges are
decorated with the heads of the supporters and charges from the two cities' arms – dragons
are flanked by swords and sable antelopes gorged with mural crowns are flanked by battery
stamps, used for crushing ore. Decorating one side of the rim are the enamelled arms of
Johannesburg, which had been newly registered by the College of Arms, along with the
dates 1939 and 1945.

   Gold, a major product of South Africa, is found in abundance in the area of
Johannesburg, at the northern end of the Witwatersrand Basin. It was discovered in the
1880s and Johannesburg was founded soon thereafter. South Africa played a major role in
the War effort, providing both service personnel and a way-station for troop movements to
and from India and the Far East.

   The salver was probably designed in-house by Mappin & Webb but to a closely detailed
requirement of the South African patrons. Its clean, sharp look reflects the aspirations of
the increasingly influential Council of Industrial Design, founded by Hugh Dalton in 1944,
which eventually became the Design Council and contributed to the Festival of Britain,
held in 1951.

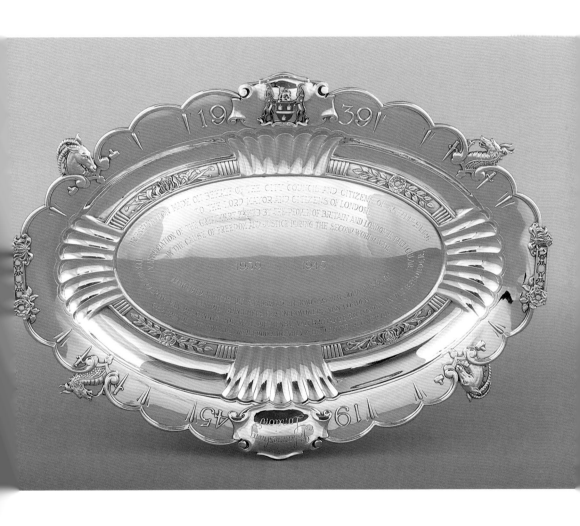

73

An equestrian model of H.R.H. the Princess Elizabeth

Modelled by Doris Lindner, London Assay Office mark for 1952–53
Silver-gilt, 53.3 cm high, unknown weight
Presented by Sir Leslie Boyce, Bt (LM 1951–52)

In June 1951 Princess Elizabeth took the salute at the Trooping of the Colour at Horse
Guards Parade in place of her father, King George VI, who was unwell. Princess Elizabeth,
just twenty-five years old, is shown wearing the uniform and tricorn hat of a Colonel of
the Grenadier Guards to salute their Colour. She rides Winston, a bay police-horse foaled in
1937, who was bought by the Mounted Branch of the Metropolitan Police Service in 1944, a
year in which all horses acquired had names beginning with W. Winston was first ridden
at a Trooping by George VI in 1947 and Queen Elizabeth II rode him after her accession
until he was retired in 1956.

Shown in a position of rest, Winston has his right foreleg extended and neck gracefully
arched, while the Princess, riding side-saddle, gazes intently into the left distance.
Modelled by Doris Lindner and apparently unique, this was nevertheless the second model
the artist had made depicting the Princess on horseback; the first was in 1947, when,
mounted on Tommy, Elizabeth rode behind the King at the Trooping of the Colour of the
Coldstream Guards, wearing Battle Dress. The earlier sculpture was made for a porcelain
model of the Worcester manufactory and published in a limited edition of a hundred the
following year. Lindner, one of the most distinguished animal sculptors of her generation,
worked for Worcester until the 1970s, specializing in horses and farm animals. This silver
model is signed by Lindner but, as she was not a silversmith and therefore had no mark, it
bears only the London Assay Office mark for 1952–53.

Sir Leslie Boyce was born in Australia. After distinguished service during the First
World War he settled in England, read law at Balliol College, Oxford, and ran a number
of engineering companies before becoming a Unionist MP in 1929, entering City life in
the 1940s. Keen to foster warm relationships with the Dominions, particularly his own of
Australia, his austere Lord Mayor's Show paused at Australia House in the Strand so that he
could receive a message of goodwill from Robert Menzies, the Australian Prime Minister,
a compliment returned when Sir Leslie conferred the Freedom of the City on Menzies
the following year. This silver model of Princess Elizabeth encapsulates the loyalty to
the Crown of the City and the Dominions. The recent London Declaration of 1949, which
effectively founded the Commonwealth of Nations, resonates in the gift of this youthful
figure with the hopes for its future.

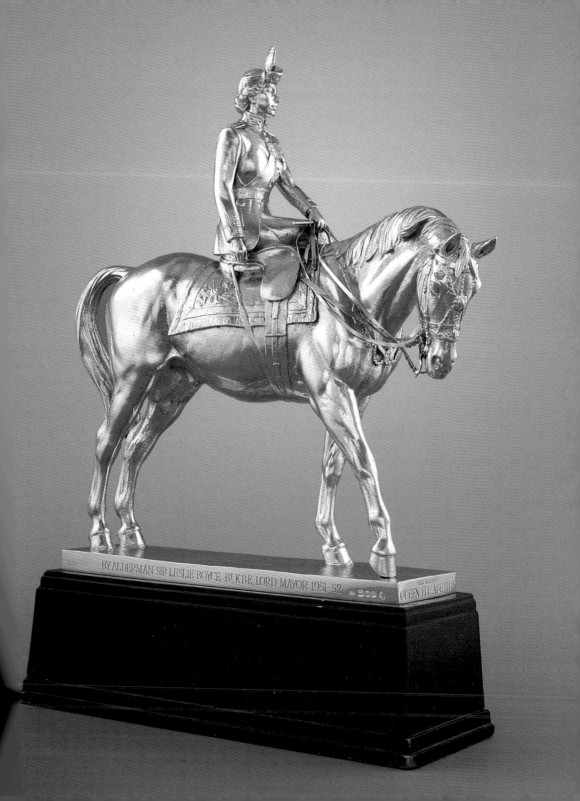

BY ALDERMAN SIR LESLIE BOYCE, Bt. KBE, LORD MAYOR 1951-52   HER MAJESTY QUEEN ELIZABETH II

74

The Portuguese Soup Tureen and Stand

Lisbon silver marks
Silver, the stand 72.3 cm long, the tureen 30.5 cm high, 10637 gm gross
Presented by the President of Portugal, Francisco Craveiro Lopes, to the City, 1955

Though this magnificent tureen and stand are to a highly elaborate French Rococo design, the model is actually far more likely to be from London than Paris. French silver of the mid eighteenth century was greatly influential, particularly in Portugal, where João V, using his vast wealth from the colony of Brazil, imported luxury goods from France. Thomas Germain and his son François-Thomas Germain, the famous silversmiths to Louis XV, provided several services to the Portuguese court and made the Rococo style fashionable throughout Europe. However, the long, low form of this replica, and the gadrooned body and stylized foliage scrolls, are more English than French; the French generally emphasized naturalistic elements and used a more rounded form of tureen, the *pot à oille*. Placed on the table for guests to serve themselves, tureens of this form acted as centrepieces and expressions of wealth as well as practical service wares. A model by John Parker and Edward Wakelin of about 1760 is the most likely source. The central cartouche is cast with the City arms.

Air Force General Francisco Craveiro Lopes was elected twelfth President of the Portuguese Republic in 1951. He showed cautious detachment from the government of Prime Minister Antonio de Oliviera Salazar, virtual dictator of Portugal from 1932 to 1968. Lopes worked hard to mend relationships with Europe after Portugal declared neutrality during the Second World War, not least with Britain, the country's oldest ally. President Lopes arrived by sea on his State visit to Britain, which began on 25 October 1955, and was greeted by the Queen and Prince Phillip at Westminster Pier. The following day President and Senhora Lopes drove to the Guildhall for a reception in the Library by the Lord Mayor Sir Seymour Howard, the Sheriffs, Aldermen and Common Council, before a luncheon in the Hall. At the conclusion of the welcoming ceremony, two top-hatted City servants carried this tureen and salver down the length of the Library for presentation by the President to the Lord Mayor.

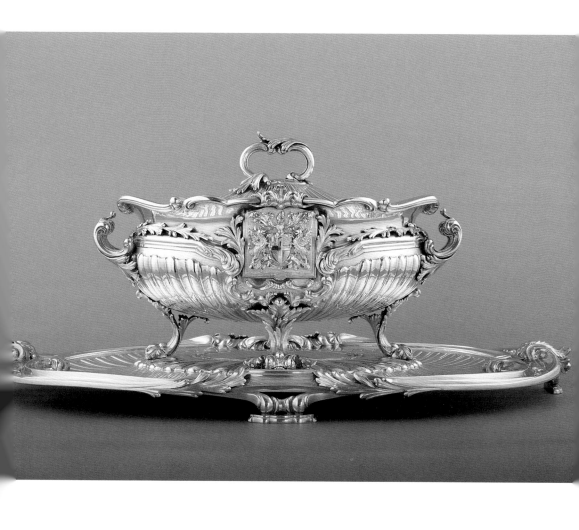

75

The Hoare Cups and Covers

Atholl Hill for Wakely & Wheeler, London, 1962–63 and 1963–64
Silver-gilt and silver, 35.5 cm high, 3172 gm gross
Presented by the Worshipful Company of Goldsmiths to Sir Frederick Hoare (LM 1961–62)
and presented by him to the Mansion House plate collection

Sir Frederick Hoare was a member of one of several London dynasties who provided
Aldermen and Lord Mayors for the City over several centuries. The Hoare family were
goldsmiths and bankers, first at the sign of the Golden Bottle in Cheapside, then, more
famously, from their house in Fleet Street, which is still the bank's head office. The oldest
bank in the United Kingdom, it was founded in 1672 by Sir Richard Hoare (LM 1712–13).
His second son, also called Richard Hoare, followed him into City life (LM 1745–46). Two
hundred years later, Sir Frederick Hoare, chairman of the bank and a member of the
Goldsmiths' Company, was elected Lord Mayor in 1961. His livery company then presented
him with these magnificent cups, designed by the Scottish silversmith Atholl Hill. Sir
Frederick was a long-serving member of the Court of Assistants of the Goldsmiths'
Company and their Prime Warden in 1966–67.

Two cones are lightly engraved with vertical striations, one inverted on to the other to
form the basis of the design, the bottom cone extended from within the base to form a
simple foot. The upper cone extends vertically to add volume to the body of the drinking
vessel. Three angular handles join the two parts of the cups, while at the narrow waist
three fretwork plaques in silver, curved to follow the lines of the cones, show the arms of
the City, of Hoare and of the Goldsmiths' Company. Flat lids with thin, tapered spikes
as knops are set with lozenges engraved with the three crests of the arms below. The
bases were extensions to the original design, added to allow the inclusion of dedicatory
inscriptions, but they in no way detract from the overall unity of the design.

Hill, from Dundee, trained at the Glasgow School of Design. His several ecclesiastical
commissions might have influenced the model of these 'loving cups' in a distinctly chalice-
like shape. However, the three handles differentiate the use, being made to be passed
from hand to hand, always leaving a handle free if passed using both hands. Though Sir
Frederick had been given them by his livery company, he chose to present the cups to the
Mansion House plate collection, as the inscribed bases record.

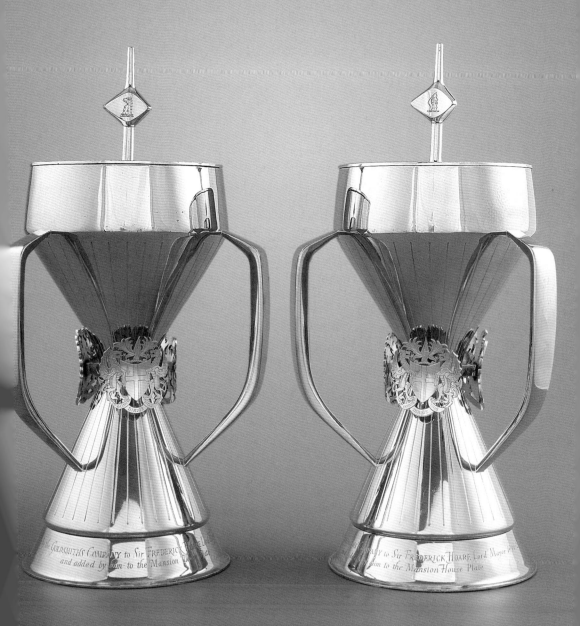

76

A pair of fruit dishes

Anthony Elson for Carrington & Co., London, 1964–65
Silver-gilt, 28.5 cm diameter, 19.7 cm high, 3048 gm
Presented by Sir Bernard Waley-Cohen, Bt (LM 1960–61)

Sir Bernard Waley-Cohen was a thorough-going City man and public servant, though
his heart lay in rural pursuits in Devonshire. A director of Lloyds Bank for many years,
from 1936 he was a liveryman of the Clothworkers' Company, becoming Master in 1975.
Alderman for Portsoken Ward, he was elected Lord Mayor in 1960, followed by attachments
to a large number of educational and charitable bodies, not least University College,
London. At the conclusion of his year he commissioned this pair of dishes, following in a
long tradition of making a gift to the Mansion House plate collection on leaving office.

Bernard Copping, director of the manufacturing silversmiths William Comyns Ltd,
asked Anthony Elson to join the firm after seeing his graduate show at the Royal College
of Art. Elson was then aged twenty-eight. To commission these dishes Waley-Cohen went
to Carringtons, who in turn asked Comyns for ideas, who in turn asked Elson for designs
– demonstrating just how far commissions can travel from patron to designer. Elson had
won a silver medal for geometric design at the R.C.A. and that skill is clear in the slightly
tapering diapered stems. The broad bowls – their finely hammered surface, with echoes of
handicraft – and the low, domed bases are perfectly in tune with the new aesthetic of the
1960s. The arms of the City have been cast, chased and applied. The rich, deep gilding adds
considerable dignity to the simple forms. Elson's design was made by Comyns, though
they are marked by Carringtons as retailer. Elson is an active member of the Goldsmiths'
Company – he was Chairman of their Council for Craft – and has gone on to provide many
pieces on commission for livery companies, universities and corporations.

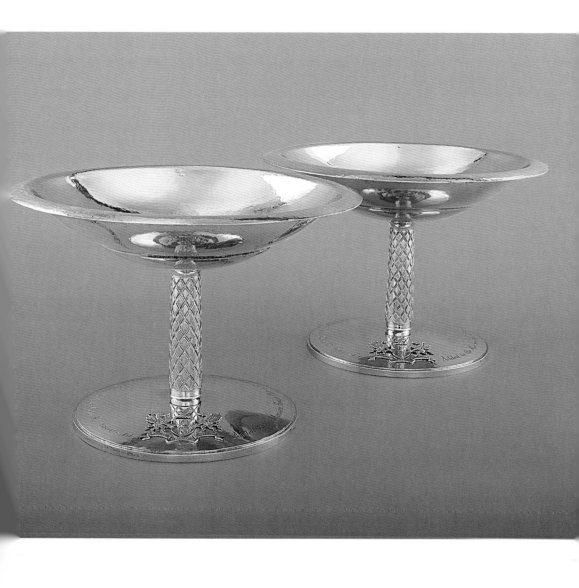

77

The Ackroyd Cup and Cover

Hicklenton & Phillips, London, 1964–65
Silver-gilt, 48.2 cm high, 975 gm
Presented by Sir Cuthbert Ackroyd, Bt (LM 1955–56)

This elegant, dignified and undecorated ovoid cup and cover, standing on a simple,
baluster foot and stem, is surmounted by a scale replica of the steeple of the Church of
St Mary-le-Bow in Cheapside, where hang the famous Bow bells. Second only to St Paul's
Cathedral amongst City churches, it is named for the arches or 'bows' of its ancient
structure, built in 1091 after the Saxon church was destroyed by a tornado. A 'peculiarity'
of the Archdiocese of Canterbury and under its direct authority, it is home to the Court of
Arches. The bells were made famous when they stopped Dick Whittington in his tracks at
Highgate and he returned to London, becoming Lord Mayor three times over. To be born
within their sound is apparently the sign of a true Cockney. The Norman church was
destroyed in the Great Fire, rebuilt to the designs of Sir Christopher Wren and completed
in 1680. The tower is a masterful architectural exercise – moving from a square to a circle to
a pyramid, proportionately, with fluidity and ease. The steeple, 68 metres high, was rebuilt
a third time after damage during the Blitz, in May 1941. The bells, having been destroyed
by the fire, were recast in 1956 by Mears & Stainbank at the Whitechapel Foundry.

Sir Cuthbert Ackroyd, from Dewsbury in Yorkshire, Alderman for the Ward of
Cordwainer in which St Mary's stands, was also their churchwarden and deeply involved
in the post-War rebuilding and the recasting of the famous ring of bells, twelve in all.
The bells were eventually hung and rung again in 1961, when this cup was commissioned
by the former Lord Mayor and presented to the Mansion House plate collection in 1964.
Inscriptions on the body record that gift, and on the foot record Sir Cuthbert's role in the
restoration of St-Mary-le-Bow.

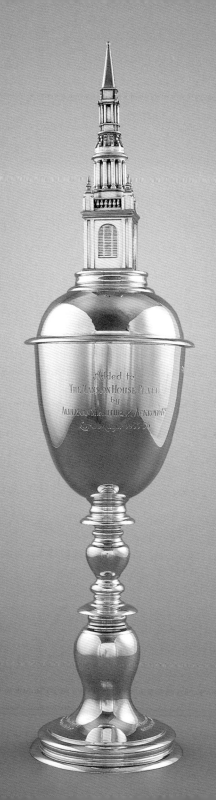

78

The Denny Centrepiece

Wakely & Wheeler, London, 1968–69
Silver and silver-gilt, 33 cm diameter, 5 cm high, 1648 gm
Presented by Sir Lionel Denny (LM 1965-66)

This centrepiece is designed to hold flowers within the divaricated sun-rays of the removable ring that stands on tubular legs in the shallow circular bowl, or it can be used simply as a table decoration, unadorned. The variety of textures and the angular forms all date the design to the late 1960s. Though the designer for Wakely & Wheeler is unrecorded, Gerald Benney is a name that springs to mind as an influence. He studied under Dunstan Pruden at Brighton College of Art, where his father was principal, and then under Robert Goodden at the Royal College of Art in the early 1950s. Benney himself was greatly influenced by the purity and minimalism of Scandinavian design. The bark texture of the interior ring and the shallow circular shape of the present bowl are particularly consistent with Benney's designs.

In the centre of the bowl is a pierced sheet of silver, fixed to the base by another tube-like support, cut and engraved in a highly linear and stylized form, with the arms of the donor, Sir Lionel Denny. Alderman for Billingsgate Ward, Sir Lionel was Master of all three of his livery companies – the Barber-Surgeons, the Vintners and the Watermen and Lightermen. A fruit importer by trade, he made fruit the theme of his Lord Mayor's Show. The inscription round the vertical edge of the bowl records the donation in a fine Roman-style font, very similar to Eric Gill's Perpetua. Dunstan Pruden was the silversmith at the Guild of St Joseph, founded by Gill.

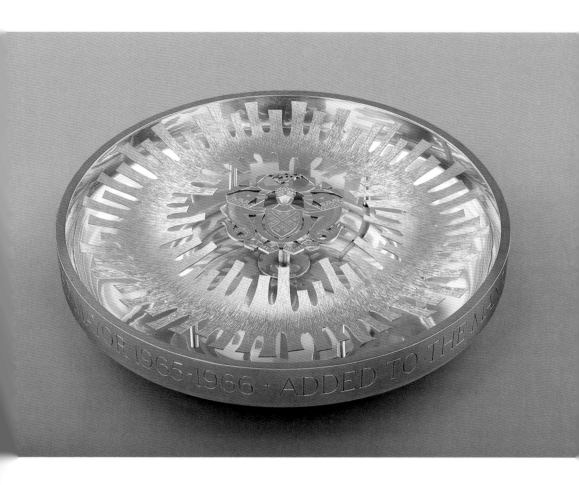

79

The Miller Cup and Cover

Hamilton & Inches, Edinburgh, 1969–70
Silver-gilt and a cairngorm, 38.7 cm high, 3589 gm
Presented by Sir James Miller (LM 1964–65)

It is entirely appropriate that Sir James Miller – an architect and civil engineer born in
Edinburgh, where he had been the Lord Provost from 1951 until 1954 – should present
a replica of a Scottish mether, or loving cup, to the Mansion House plate collection at
the conclusion of his Mayoral year. Ancient examples of methers, Gaelic in origin, are
carved whole from oak, yew or alder, with the characteristic arms dropping to the base
and forming feet. Used for drinking mead (fermented honey and water) at feasts, where
large examples would be passed from guest to guest, they were also used for storage or for
measuring tithes. Some have long histories, like the Dunvegan Cup, a fifteenth-century
mether of wood mounted with silver plaques and bands, an heirloom of the Clan Macleod
preserved at Dunvegan Castle on the Isle of Skye.

The tankard shape of this example is slightly flared, with three auricular handles
rising from the body, touching it again at the base and thinning towards pad feet. The
simple domed lid is set with a large faceted cairngorm, a yellowish-brown form of smoky
quartz found in the Cairngorm Mountains of central Scotland. The revival of interest in
ancient Scottish art forms was greatly encouraged by the works of Sir Walter Scott in the
early nineteenth century, and further inspired by the Great Exhibition of 1851 and the
reproduction of Gaelic treasures of metalwork that led the Celtic Revival in the 1890s.
Methers in silver and other metals have become popular forms for presentation cups
and Christening presents, forgetting their original function – to enable consumption of
alcohol in large quantities. Hamilton & Inches, one of Scotland's foremost manufacturers
and retailers of silver, was founded in Edinburgh in 1866 and continues to make replicas of
historic Scottish forms, particularly the flattened double-handled drinking cups known as
quaishes.

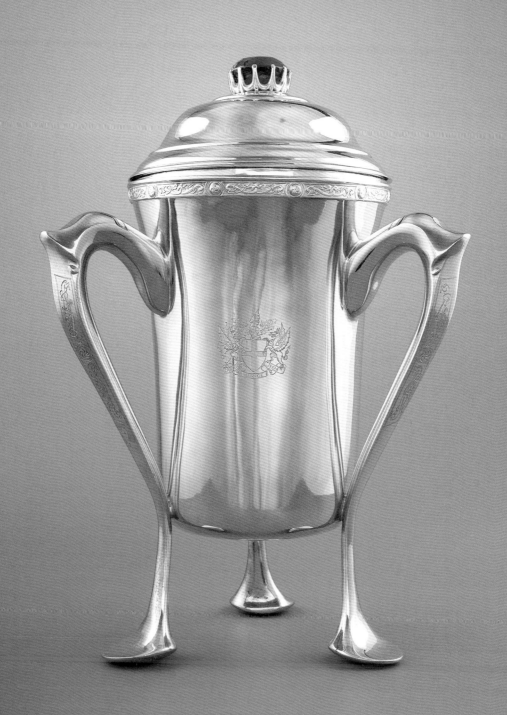

80

A lectern and speech timer

LECTERN Leslie Durbin, London, 1971–72; silver, gilt-metal and Perspex
Presented by Sir Gilbert Inglefield (LM 1967-8), Sir Ian Bowater (LM 1969-70)
and Sir Peter Studd (LM 1970—71)
SPEECH TIMER Alex Styles for Garrard & Co., London, 1977–78; silver-gilt,
glass and coloured sands, 26.5 cm high, 2205 gm including the glass
Presented by Sir Lindsay Ring (LM 1975-76)

A speech can on occasions / Bring eternity to mind,
But to measure such misfortune / This gift was not designed.

Sir Lindsay Ring's short three-stanza poem engraved on the top of this timer ends by reminding speakers that *Short speeches can be best.* And he should have known. He was chairman of the famous City catering company Ring & Brymer (Birch) Ltd, founded by a Mr Horton in the reign of George I and acquired by Lucas Birch in the mid eighteenth century. Lucas and his son Samuel Birch (LM 1814-15) built up a thriving catering business for civic and livery banquets, with turtle soup their speciality. In 1836 Samuel sold the business to Ring & Brymer, who retained the historic name of Birch in parenthesis. Sir Lindsay Ring in turn sold the company to Lord Forte in 1962, but he remained as chairman for many years. In his position as an Alderman of the Ward of Bishopsgate and master of his livery, the Armourers and Brasiers' Company, he must have lived through hundreds if not thousands of over-long speeches, which this machine was intended to prevent in an elegant but obvious way, with its intentionally large and eye-catching message.

Alex Styles's design was closely supervised by Sir Lindsay and allows for speeches to be timed by three glasses – with white sand for a normal-length speech, yellow as a warning, and red to indicate the speech is over-long and must stop. Sadly, the red timer has become clogged. The octagonal case has bands of bark-textured decoration at top and bottom, typical of Styles's work. Trained at the Central School of Arts and Crafts, he became a staff designer for the Goldsmiths & Silversmiths Co. in 1947 before moving to Garrard & Co. in 1952. He designed a large amount of civic, university and corporate plate, insignia in particular. He retired from Garrards in 1982.

Presented by a trio of Lord Mayors, the achingly simple lectern, with the City arms gilded on the Perspex, was designed by Leslie Durbin, who had trained in the workshop of Omar Ramsden (nos. 66 and 69) and made the Sword of Stalingrad designed by Reginald Gleadowe (see no. 68), which neatly emphasizes the continuation of great designers in the Mansion House plate collection. The elegant lectern may have inspired the lengthy speeches Sir Lindsey Ring subsequently aimed to curb. It was joined by a replica companion in the year of Sir Roger Gifford (LM 2012-13).

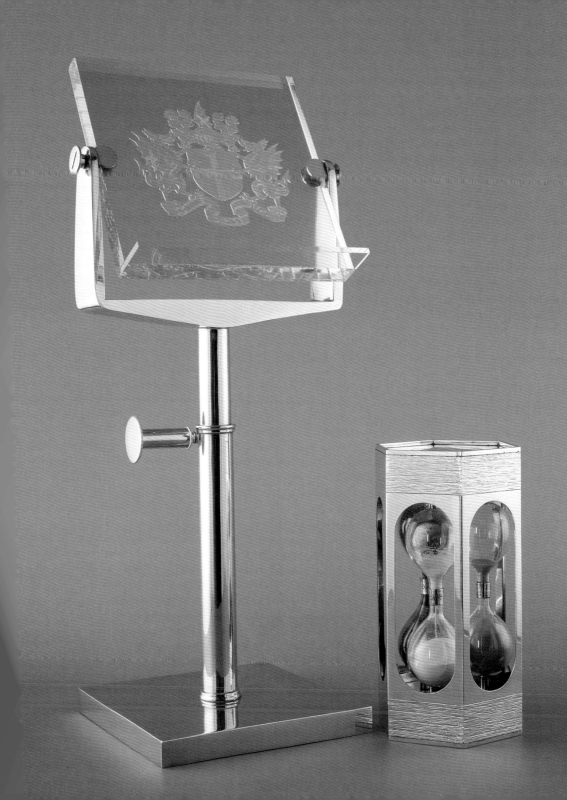

81

Models of a Pikeman and a Musketeer of the H.A.C.

PIKEMAN M.P. Levine, London, 1999–2000. Silver and silver-gilt, 65 cm high
Presented by Lord Levine of Portsoken (LM 1998–99)
MUSKETEER M.P. Levine, London, 1999–2000. Silver and silver-gilt, 44.5 cm high
Presented by Alderman Clive Martin (LM 1999–2000), later Sir Clive Martin

Founded by Henry VIII in 1537 by Royal Charter, the Honourable Artillery Company is
the oldest regiment of the British Army and the second most senior unit of the Territorial
Army. Artillery House by Bunhill Fields, just north of the City, was acquired in 1641 as
the headquarters of the Company and continues in use to this day. During the Civil War,
the Treasurer took the Company's silver into safekeeping and its return is still awaited. In
1925 the H.A.C. formed the Company of Pikemen and Musketeers to take part in the Royal
Tournament, held at the Royal Agricultural Hall in Islington. When this proved a great
success, the demonstration team were kept together and, dressed in copies of seventeenth-
century uniforms with period weapons, they now provide colour and pageantry at events
in the City of London and elsewhere, acting as the Lord Mayor's Guard on ceremonial
occasions. Members are drawn from veterans of the H.A.C.

These silver figures represent the two types of soldiers of the Company, which, as well
as wearing period uniform, still uses a number of seventeenth-century commands. Drawn
from William Bariffe's 1635 treatise *Military Discipline or, The Young Artillery Man*, the
pikeman – holding what in life-size would be a twelve-foot-long weapon tipped by a steel
leaf-shaped blade with a tasselled guard – has followed the order to 'Assume a lazy posture'.
He wears half-armour of a back- and breast-plate, joined by pauldrons with tassets below
that have sliding rivets to allow for movement and protect the upper legs. On his head he
wears an oval-brimmed morion, which in life is trimmed with red ostrich feathers. His
tunic and breeches would also be Venetian red, the quantity and quality of linen and lace
denoting rank. The model of the musketeer carries a musket and rest, used to support the
heavy gun when aiming and firing. He wears the typical wide-brimmed black felt hat with
feathers, surcoat (which would be buff coloured) and a bandolier over the shoulder, from
which are suspended twelve cartridges, called 'Apostles', a power horn and a priming flask.
The Royal Warrant granted in 1955 allows the Company to parade no more than 63 men at
any one time, that being the size of a company in the seventeenth century.

Presented by two consecutive Lord Mayors in 2000, both figures bear the Millennium
hallmark, being made by M.P. Levene, Lord Levene's family firm. Both donors have close
ties with the armed services. Lord Levene was Hon. Colonel of the Royal Corps of Transport
and a member of the Court of Assistants of the H.A.C. for many years, while Sir Clive was
Regimental Colonel of the H.A.C. and Master Gunner of the Tower of London, where the
H.A.C. has the honour of firing royal salutes.

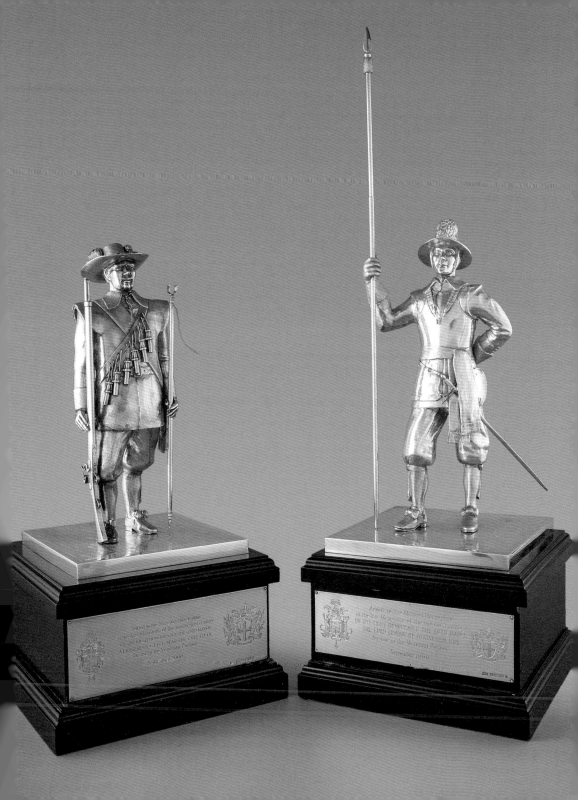

82

A model of the al Masmak Fort, Riyadh

Unknown maker, The Philippines, c. 2007, retailed by Mouawad
Silver-gilt, mother-of-pearl, malachite, 52 cm long, 38 cm wide, unknown weight
Presented by King Abdullah of Saudi Arabia, 2007

Riyadh's ancient al Masmak Fort, ancestral seat of the Saud family, represented here in
precious materials, acquired an almost mythical status in the history of the establishment
of Saudi rule when recaptured in 1902 by the first king, Abdulaziz. Offered by his son King
Abdullah of Saudi Arabia to the Mansion House plate collection during his State visit in
October 2007, it joins a distinguished group of gifts from royal and presidential visitors.
Brick-and-daub-built, with four round tapering crenellated towers, the fort is here
replicated in detail and includes silver-gilt palm-trees standing on a base of malachite
and mother-of-pearl. Entered by a single gateway set with a small door that only allows
the access of one person at a time, the original fort is now a museum.

Receiving heads of state during official visits has become part of the repertoire of the
Lord Mayor's year. Their gifts to the City over the years have included magnificent silver
vases of Meiji-period design presented by Emperor Hirohito of Japan in 1971, a tureen and
stand from the Portuguese president in 1974 (no. 74), and a traditional double-handled
bowl from the Bailiff and States of Jersey in 1997. Loved or loathed, this model was made by
Philippine craftsmen for the distinguished firm of Lebanese jewellers Mouawad, founded
in Beirut in 1890 but now based in Geneva in its fourth generation. Apparently another
example was presented to H.M. the Queen on the same State visit. Nowadays, acquisitions
to the Mansion House plate collection are rarely necessities, and gifts such as these are
more decorative and symbolic than useful, however valuable. Even so, mementoes are still
very happily received by the City's Lord Mayors.

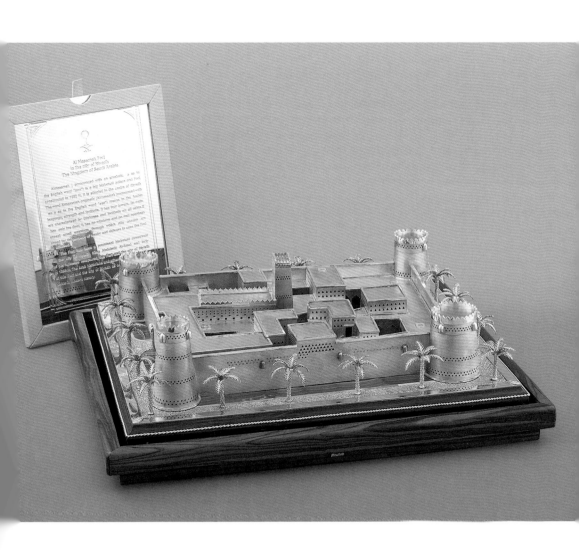

Acknowledgements

This book was produced with the support and collaboration of the staff of the
Guildhall Art Gallery, the Mansion House and the London Metropolitan Archives,
City of London.

SPONSORS

Agincourt 600
The City of London
The Worshipful Company of Goldsmiths
Hazlitt Ltd
The Capelain Collection

THANKS TO

The Rt Hon the Lord Mayor and Lady Mayoress, Alderman Alan and Mrs Gilly Yarrow,
and Nala; Andrew Ford, Toby Allen and Abderrazzak Sakim at the Mansion House
plate collection; William Chapman, James North, Adam Rout, Wayne Garrigan
and Colin Tucker at Mansion House; Philippa Glanville, Sir Christopher Collett,
Bt, Peter Kane, Christopher Bilsland, Clare Scott, Sabine Schlosser, Ross Garcia,
Rosie Mills, John Morton Morris, John Dennis, Dean Maisey, Christopher Maxwell,
Jasper Mordhorst, Robert Lane, Robyn Mercer, Luke Schrager, Clare Chapman, Mike
Barford, Brian Duffy, Anthony Elson, our editors Laura Parker and Paul Holberton,
Christopher Breyne, Fiona Jennison-Marr and Sir Roger Gifford. A special thankyou
to Seamus McKenna for his wonderful photography.

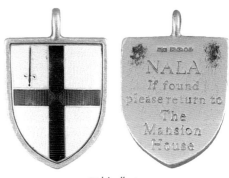

Nala's collar tag
Grant McDonald, silver and enamel, 2014
Presented to Alan Yarrow LM 2014–15